What people are saying

Very few books are as honest an[...] [...]out the journey of pain and hope undergone by those who lose a child. Ian and Rosi have done us a huge service in sharing, with no holds barred, what it was like to live the experience of the death of their student daughter Esther. This is a book for all of us – whether we're on that journey ourselves or supporting others. Above all, it's a story of trusting and faith in God in the midst of grief.

Pete Broadbent, Bishop of Willesden & Deputy Bishop of London.

No parent should have to watch their child die. Rosi and Ian White did. They have now had the courage to write about their experience and do so with an openness and honesty that is compelling. This is not an easy read. However, the warmth, tenderness, raw emotion and wit with which this is written will allow the reader a glimpse into a family held together by love for one another. This love runs deep because it is fuelled by God's love for them and no trite or easy answers are offered. This is one family's story of finding God's love and faithfulness in the midst of intense sadness and loss. There is hope in this journey. My prayer is that many will find this book helpful whether journeying with grief personally or standing alongside others in their walk through a dark valley.

Elaine Duncan, Chief Executive of the Scottish Bible Society.

No one chooses the path that Ian and Rosi have had to walk. The sadness of losing someone you love unexpectedly is so consuming that there are times when you feel like you are falling headlong into a very dark and very deep well. Through their openness, vulnerability and honesty, Ian and Rosi throw a lifeline into the well. As I read their words I wept. They have fallen into the well of despair and loss but they have not drowned. Instead, their words offer real hope that God is with us in the darkest and deepest of our despair and that He will not abandon us. I am sure this book will help many people who feel utterly abandoned by God. To describe it as beautiful is to do it an injustice. I feel more hope because of their words. My faith is strengthened. Thank God for 'The Road Not Chosen' and for the powerful witness of the White family.

Malcolm Duncan, Author & Senior Minister of Gold Hill Baptist Church.

Dear Ian and Rosi, just to say how incredibly moved we were reading the sample of your book - it made us cry on every page, and we felt the Holy Spirit really speaking to us. It's passing like wildfire round the church family. Extremely readable - can't wait for the whole book proper. Much love,

Susie Marriott

About the authors:

Ian and Rosalyn White live in Eastbourne, U.K. and have had two children, Christopher and Esther.

Ian began his career as a research mathematician working on the staff of Swansea University and then British Petroleum. In the 1980s he studied Theology with a view to becoming a church leader and is now Senior Minister of Victoria Baptist Church in Eastbourne. He is a conference speaker, broadcaster and a keen photographer. He is also a classically trained pianist, collects rare tea from all over the world and is fascinated by the technical side of just about anything.

Rosalyn is a Social Worker with East Sussex County Council. She specialises in assessing people with complex health or social care needs and investigates safeguarding cases where vulnerable adults may be at risk. She has a passion for the pastoral side of church ministry, and in any remaining spare time she loves creating scrapbooks.

Pictures

You can view pictures which relate to key moments in the book and read about events connected with *The Road Not Chosen* on this page:

www.whites.me.uk/TheRoadNotChosen

THE

ROAD

NOT

CHOSEN

A tale of hope in the face of loss

by Ian and Rosalyn White

Published by Dr. Ian White.

Printed by Berforts Ltd., www.berfort.co.uk

First published November 2015

British Library Cataloguing-in-Publication Data:

A catalogue record for this book is available from the British Library.

ISBN: 978-0-9934534-0-3

Thank you

We owe a debt of gratitude to the people who played a pivotal role in bringing you this book. Ali Hull, whom you can find at www.writersessentials.com, painstakingly edited the manuscript and gave us consistently wise advice during the writing and publication process. Jeanette Walter has brought her attention to detail to the book too. Then there are the members of Victoria Baptist Church, many of whom encouraged us to persevere with telling our story.

Thank you to all of you.

Ian and Rosi

Table of Contents

Introduction 1

1 Bombshell 5

2 Roller-coaster 23

3 Strangeness 43

4 On View 61

5 Good Grief? 81

6 Esther's Journey 109

7 Developing Faith 125

8 Pain, the Uninvited Guest 141

9 Cambodia 161

10 Mysteries 181

11 Hope 189

Postscript 215

Heaven Day 219

Bible verses for you to think about ... 223

Additional Resources 233

Introduction

"Are we nearly there, Daddy?"

Esther's five-year-old voice rang out confidently from the back seat. We were heading off on our annual family holiday with the car loaded to the gunnels with clothes, toys, camping kit and even a small kitchen sink. Quite understandably our daughter was asking for a progress report on the journey. How much of it had we already driven and how much was still to come? In reality we had been driving for less than half a mile! What struck me about her curiosity was her childlike concept of the journey. In her young mind she had no comprehension of the distance or complexity of the journey. No idea about its twists and turns, no concept of its length or duration. All she knew was that something worth having lay at the end of it.

Grieving is like that journey. When we are thrown into grief's whirlpool we have no idea how many twists and turns it may take, no awareness of the length of the journey or how difficult it may become along the way. This book is our experience of such a journey. You may be reading it out of curiosity or because you are on this journey yourself. But wherever you're coming from, our hope is that you will find the retelling of our experience a source of help and hope.

When a child enters a family there is a long list of aspirations that arrive with them. Some of these longings are very obvious while others hover deep in the recesses of our minds where we may not even be aware of them. One of our own aspirations was to see our children successfully into adulthood and launched into independence as rounded and well-adjusted people. There were some things we really hoped and prayed our children would have, such as a deep love for God. As Christians that has always been high on our personal agenda and we hoped it would be on theirs too.

As parents, the two of us had slightly different emphases when it came to our hopes for our children, Christopher and Esther. Rosi saw creativity and people skills high on her list. She longed for them to be able to express themselves artistically and to forge deep relationships with the people in their world. Ian was keen that they developed a love for music and science. As a research scientist himself, he was enthusiastic about helping his children to understand the world around them through a scientific lens.

Above all we sought to provide a safe and loving environment with lots of encouragement. Trying to force our children into a particular mould would have resulted in frustration and disappointment. In reality we were delighted to see their very different personalities emerge as time went on.

One subconscious expectation of most parents is that our children will outlive us and even look after us in our dotage! But as we were to discover, life doesn't come with any guarantees. To the casual observer, we had a perfect family. Two parents and 2.4 children (the .4 being our pet rabbit), good prospects and excellent health. There was a sense of privilege we felt about our situation and we were enormously grateful to God for it. We tried not to take life for granted.

Neither of us expected to be arranging Esther's funeral.

This book is about our journey. We want to be honest with you about its twists and turns, the moments we triumphed and the moments we flopped. When five-year-old Esther asked about how long there was to travel before we reached our destination, we couldn't give an answer her young mind would be able to comprehend. Our journey of grief is no

Introduction

different. Our heavenly Father doesn't always give us the answers we desire and, even if He did, it is more than likely they would be beyond our human understanding. But He does travel with us on the journey and we trust there will be something worth having at the end of it.

We want this to be a story of hope, not only about our Christian hope of one day seeing Esther again, but also about hope in this life when we are faced with tragic loss. In the Bible, Paul wrote to some Christians experiencing a similar situation and said "... but we do not grieve as those who have no hope".

By reading this story we hope that will be your experience too.

1

Bombshell

Ian

I t was a Sunday which was both entirely normal and entirely abnormal. I was standing on a platform facing several hundred people, preaching about a passage from the Bible and doing my best to show its relevance for their lives. For me that is normality. But in the previous week something unexpected had happened which made this sermon entirely abnormal. One of the almost uncanny aspects of studying the Bible is those occasions when God gives a message to communicate that, while being related to the passage, is rather left-of-field. I've come to accept these moments as a prompting from God's Holy Spirit and this one had happened on Thursday.

The text I was expounding was an incident when Christ came face to face with death (John 11:1-45). Jesus had received a message that a close friend of His called Lazarus was seriously ill a couple of miles away, and He was being asked to come and pray for him before the worst happened. Uncharacteristically, Jesus delayed setting out so by the time He arrived at the town, His friend had already died and been buried. The sadness of the occasion brought Jesus to tears and prompted one of His greatest sayings: "I am the resurrection and the life. He who believes in me will live, even though he dies" (John 11:25). My initial preparation was leading me to focus on this great "I am" statement of Jesus. But the more I prayed and studied, the more I had a hunch that I should take a different direction and focus on the grieving of Mary and Martha in the wake of losing their brother Lazarus. I ended up preparing to preach on "Grieving with hope – handling grief with heaven in view."

My study door opened and Rosi breezed in, brandishing a steaming mug of coffee.

"This should keep the brain cells going," she quipped.

Next to my mouse was a mug mat Esther had made as a child, proudly bearing the initial D for Daddy. Rosi replaced an empty mug with the new drink.

"By the way, have you heard from Esther today?"

"Nope."

"Ah well," she shrugged and turned to leave. "I just keep getting her voicemail."

Sunday came and I preached to the usual congregations but I had no idea that something else was happening at the same time.

I was preaching to myself.

Rosi

Christmas presents from your children are always precious, even if they are small. It's the love in which they are packaged that gives them a value that is often way beyond their cost. Esther, who was a university student in Glasgow, Scotland, had asked what I wanted for Christmas. But being so far away from each other, we weren't able to meet up, go browsing in the local shops and find something that had meaning for us both. In the end, it was all done over the internet. I couldn't think of anything I needed at the time so I suggested she bought me a book.

"But which book, Mum?" she said. "You'll have to give me *some* idea." I particularly enjoy remarkable stories about Christians who have overcome adversity. So it was while we were simultaneously surfing through the pages of Wesley Owen's site from opposite ends of the country that I came across *90 Minutes in Heaven* by Don Piper.

"That will do nicely," I said to her.

"OK, Mum." And by Christmas the book had arrived.

By February I had absorbed its remarkable story and found its message hovering around in the back of my mind. Ian and I were enjoying an idle moment together one Saturday morning, I was tidying and he was fixing something. In a pile I came across the book.

"Ian, you must read this," I urged, tossing it into the air for him to catch.

"Yeah, OK," he said distractedly, his tone of voice telling me it probably wasn't going to happen.

"It's weird, but we haven't heard from Esther again today."

"Oh don't worry! She's probably forgotten to charge up her phone again. You know what she's like!"

"Hmm. I hope you're right."

That book was to become my daughter's final present to me before she entered the place the author was writing about. Although neither of us realised it at the time, her parting gift was a book about heaven.

The Road Not Chosen

Monday

Rosi

Esther's nightly phone calls usually came from her home in Glasgow. It was a rambling old house she shared with several other university students, and she had only been living there a few months. There was nothing unusual about her forgetting to charge her phone or just losing it somewhere in her belongings. So getting her voicemail only left me mildly curious. But when we hadn't spoken for five days, my curiosity turned to concern. Late on the Monday evening 9th February, I tried another route. In the house there was a landline the students used for their internet connection. The handset was elsewhere in the house. It was answered by Kit, one of Esther's housemates, who had recently moved in.

"Hi Kit, I'm trying to get in touch with Esther. Could you find her for me please?"

"I don't think she's been in the house today."

"Any idea where she's gone?"

"I think she went away for the weekend and I don't know if she's got back."

At this, my heart sank and my mind went into overdrive.

"Kit, I'm speaking from her home. She hasn't been here and she would usually tell me if she was on a trip. Could you go and check she's not in her room please – and don't take silence as an answer. If there's no response, just let yourself in to see if she's sleeping."

There was what seemed to be a long pause. In reality it was less than a minute but it felt like hours.

Bombshell

"Hello?" Even in that single word, Kit's voice was laden with concern. "I've found her. She's sleeping – snoring heavily in fact. She's been sick in her sleep and she's foaming at the mouth."

It took me a moment to process the enormity of what I was hearing.

"Kit, did you know she's diabetic?"

"No, I didn't know that. Is there anything I can do?"

"Yes, just call 999 and get an ambulance."

"OK – and I'll ring you back."

The line went dead.

The next hour was one of the longest of my life. I rang Ian, even though I knew he was in a church leaders' meeting.

"Hi, it's Ian White speaking. I'm sorry I can't take your call at the moment but please leave me a message after this bleep ..." It was the cheery message I'd become familiar with, but this time I didn't appreciate its joviality.

"Ian, I need your voice, not your voicemail."

The phone rang and I prepared to break the news to Ian.

"Erm. This is Mrs Cooper here. I need to talk to Dr White about my husband's funeral."

I could hardly believe my ears. With all that was going on in Glasgow, here was a lady who wanted Ian to do work for her, and at 10.30 in the evening. And she wasn't the only incoming request that night. I found myself getting rid of people as quickly as I could for fear of missing Kit's return call.

Ian arrived home and the phone rang again. This time it was Kit. Esther was deeply unconscious and it had taken four paramedics to bind her to a stretcher and manoeuvre her down the winding staircase and into the waiting ambulance. She was being taken to the Western Infirmary and we were to ring them at 1.00am. Time again stretched out like an eternity.

Ian

One a.m. came and I called the hospital.

"Oh, I'm glad you've rung," said the nurse. "All we know about this patient is her name, Esther. Do you have some connection with her?"

"Yes, I'm her father."

Somehow the idea of "this patient" being on a bed, alone and unconscious, in an Accident and Emergency department with only her first name to identify her, struck me as tragic. It was the kind of plot you might invent for a movie. But this was real life – Esther's life.

"Her name is Esther Mary White, she's twenty-two, a student, and she's an insulin dependent diabetic."

A barrage of questions followed which allowed me to put her story into perspective for the medics.

"She's very drowsy," said the nurse, "so we're transferring her to the ITU and doing a brain scan."

Mention of the ITU (Intensive Treatment Unit) reinforced the seriousness of her plight, and when the call was over I shared the news with Rosi. At that moment we did the one thing that could make a difference – we prayed. Few of our prayer moments had been as urgent as this.

The need to think practically about booking the next flight to Glasgow now took over. This was not the first time we'd supported Esther in hospital with her diabetes. The previous year she had been admitted in a hurry and Rosi had flown up to help her. But there was something from that incident that haunted me. I could still hear my wife's tears ringing in my ears as she had phoned from a park bench in Glasgow. "Ian ... I wish you were here ... I really need you ... I feel so alone."

She now looked me straight in the eyes with the kind of look that said "I am not going to take 'no' for an answer here" and said, "Ian, I just can't face it alone this time."

We snatched a few hours of fitful sleep before setting off to Scotland at the crack of dawn.

Together.

Tuesday

Ian and Rosi

Tuesday proved to be an extremely long and emotionally draining day. The Kit we had spoken with on the phone met us at the airport, his face ashen. Seeing a middle-aged couple emerge from the Gatwick flight with concern on their faces, he came over to greet us.

"Ian and Rosi White?"

"Yes. You must be Kit."

We shook hands and he fixed his gaze on us.

"Now," he said earnestly, his tone of voice indicating he wasn't expecting a discussion, "I've taken the day off work so I can be your taxi driver. I'll ferry you wherever you want to go, so you don't have to worry about public transport. I'll just sit in the car and wait for you."

He had only known our daughter for a few weeks and this unexpected kindness touched us deeply. The potential gravity of Esther's situation hadn't really sunk in and we both found ourselves on our mobiles to our offices, clearly explaining what arrangements would need to be reorganised, as if it was happening to someone completely unrelated to us. At least, Mrs Cooper would now be satisfied.

On arriving at the ITU, a nurse took us into a side room and explained that Esther was on a life support machine.

"When you go in to her," she said, "you'll see she's all wired up. I want to tell you this now so it's not too much of a shock."

Esther had been sedated to prevent further pressure on the brain. The nurse indicated this was likely to be a temporary stage until they brought her round. An X-ray seemed to show she had suffered a brain haemorrhage but the consultant would give us more information when he visited the ward. This cushioned the blow a little because initially it didn't appear to be related to Esther's diabetes.

It was beginning to sink in how seriously ill Esther was. When the nurse came past, Rosi glanced at her and said, "This is serious, isn't it?" (An inane comment for someone in an ITU!) But we needed to know how Esther's condition rated with the nurse who was experienced at treating sedated patients.

"Yes it is," she replied earnestly; and with that the reality dawned on us. If *she* thought it was serious, then it was grave indeed.

We were spared the sight of Esther's state when she had arrived at the hospital. The staff on the ward had washed her hair and brushed its entire length. In an act of tenderness, some unknown hand had plaited it, tied a tiny white bow near its end and laid it as if flowing down her pillow. It was a sign of compassion beneath the tangle of tubes and wires. It was the kind of hairstyle we remembered from years ago when she was a carefree child playing with her friends.

"Ian," Rosi whispered when the nurse was out of earshot, "when was the last time you saw her with a bow like that in her hair?"

"Can't remember."

Looking on, powerless, at her sleeping form there was a rising sense of relief that she showed no signs of pain or distress. We waited anxiously for the consultant's ward round and time seemed to take on a different perspective as we sat by her side. Minutes seemed to repeat themselves. An hour felt like three. Eventually we were called in to see the consultant who told us there was significant swelling on her brain.

"And what might that mean?" Ian asked.

"In truth," he said, looking intently at us both, "the outcome could be anywhere on a spectrum from complete recovery to not waking up. And we won't know for a while."

There was a gravity in his tone of voice and facial expression that told us that this man, with all his ITU experience, was worried. Clearly we were into unknown territory.

Rosi

I had never wanted to hear this. During the previous week, as part of my work as a social worker, I had encountered a client who had an acquired brain injury. It had left him with significant behavioural and physical problems that were having a huge impact on his life and the rest of his family. He was now utterly dependent on the people caring for him and could do almost nothing for himself. We both knew that Esther was so private and so independent a woman that she would find a life like this almost unbearable. She would not want to impose this kind of burden on anyone. That conversation with my client was very clear in my mind and I realised that recovery with severe disability was starting to feel unthinkable.

Sitting at her bedside had a surreal quality to it. Esther was having one-on-one nursing and was completely unable to communicate. I found myself having the same banter with the young nurse that we would otherwise have had with Esther herself. At the same time, we spoke to Esther as normally as we could under the presupposition that, even though she was heavily sedated, she might be able to hear us. It was curious that sitting at Esther's bedside was stressful but not distressing. We both felt that if there was any place that could nurse her back to health, it was this one. We stroked her and kissed her, told her we loved her and that whatever the outcome we would stick by her. We prayed with her and held her hand. The dignity with which the nursing staff handled her was very moving. Even though she was deeply unconscious they would still explain everything they were about to do – change a tube, move her from one side to the other – and they always addressed her by name. In the midst of the vast array of medical technology, there was tenderness.

Ian and Rosi

Our natural instinct was to stay in the ward, just to be with her. Leaving her felt like abandonment in her time of deepest need, but we were eventually exhausted and needed to rest. The duty nurse assured us she would phone immediately if there was any change in her condition, but they were not expecting a deterioration.

Bombshell

Rosi remembered she had stayed with Esther in a cheap bed and breakfast hotel near to the Infirmary some years before. So we decided to track it down and book in, if there was space. When we arrived, we discovered it had been given an extensive makeover and gone upmarket – both in décor and price. We were in no position to debate what to do, so we booked in and were shown to a basement room with a small window overlooking a cemetery. The room was pleasant, equipped with luxurious fittings, and boasted a state-of-the-art wet room.

It was the next day before Rosi realised the significance of the room itself. It had been so extensively modified that she had not noticed it was the very room she had stayed in with Esther previously. At that moment a conversation they had had came flooding back. It was Esther's 19th birthday and she was completing her gap year activities. Even though she had been offered a place at Strathclyde University, she was going through a tunnel of doubt about whether studying at university was God's will for her. Rosi talked through her sense of being guided by God when she was applying to university and explored what other options Esther might have. "But Mum, I've got no Plan B," was her instinctive response. Being anxious for reassurance, Esther rang her Dad to get his view on the dilemma. Thankfully he gave the same advice as Rosi! Mother and daughter prayed together and thereafter Esther had much more peace that studying here was in God's plan for that phase of her life. It felt curiously comforting to be staying in the room where her final decision to come to Glasgow had been taken.

Our prayer time that evening was one that we will never forget. We were confident that God could heal Esther and we both had a strong sense that we needed to hand her life over completely to Him, so that His will for her could be realised. As our voices tried to reflect our hearts, we found ourselves praying that if God wanted to receive her into His presence, then we were willing to let her go. These were tough words to pray about our daughter.

We both received a deep sense of peace as we prayed, and at that moment Ian saw a picture in his mind's eye. In this picture, Ian visualised the two of us handing Esther over to the Lord and saw her floating away from the bed where she was lying in the ITU. As she went into the distance, there was an intense sense that she was at peace and going home. Is it possible that her spirit left as we handed her over to God in those moments? We will never know this side of eternity but we are both confident that strong subjective impressions like these are sometimes our heavenly Father communicating with us.

Surprisingly we both went soundly to sleep but were wakened within the hour by the ringtone of Ian's mobile phone. It was Joan, the ITU nurse. In her gentle Scots brogue, she let us know that Esther had deteriorated rapidly and we needed to go to the hospital. Her tone of voice was calm but insistent. "Haste ye in!" she said with a quiet urgency that jolted us into action. Instantly our minds were on full alert once again and, after throwing on some clothes, we let ourselves out of the heavy front door of the hotel, and headed into the night.

Wednesday

Ian

As we walked to the hospital, we did not talk to each other. Neither of us could find words to convey what we were going through but there was a deep comfort in each other's presence. It was bitterly cold; a clear still night with a dusting of snow covering the ground. As we walked along we heard loud voices from the opposite side of the road. Guests from the restaurant where we had eaten a few hours earlier were pouring out onto the street, laughing and joking. The triviality of their raucous banter and the weight we were carrying seemed to collide across the road, and I wanted to call out to them, "My daughter's dying! My daughter's dying! It's not funny!" But what was it to them anyway?

Having reached the hospital, it did not take long for us to realise that Esther was not likely to live for much longer. The need to have the family together seemed paramount, so I rang our son Chris in Cheltenham. He knew Esther was ill and that we had travelled to see her, but he wasn't expecting a call after midnight.

"What's wrong, Dad?" he asked blearily.

"Erm ..." I couldn't think of a tender phrase to use, so I blurted out the first thing that came into my head. "Esther is dying."

It was probably a rather curt way of answering him but they were the only words I could find on the spur of the moment. At least it was the truth. Immediately his tone of voice changed and I heard an anguished Chris call out to his wife, "Polly, Esther is dying – get up, get up!"

Within minutes they had set off for Glasgow.

Ian and Rosi

We suddenly felt a wave of loneliness. Eastbourne was a plane journey away and our son and daughter-in-law were out of contact somewhere on a motorway. Everyone else was a stranger. Agnes, the student pastoral worker from Esther's church, had visited her in the afternoon and asked us to let her know if there were developments. She had been very kind to Esther in the past and, even though it was now 1.00am, we called her. Within a few minutes, her reassuring face emerged through the ITU's swing doors and we were at last able to have a sympathetic person with whom we could share these moments.

Not long afterwards Paul, a gentle doctor in a crumpled shirt, explained the situation without mincing his words.

"I'm sorry," he said, "but Esther is dying. Her heartbeat and blood pressure are excessive and her body will not be able to sustain this for much longer."

He appeared nervous as he explained that he would be removing the ventilator and some of the other tubes. It felt as if the decision had already been made, and he was seeking reassurance that we agreed with him. This was a deep dilemma for us as Chris and Polly were still travelling, and Paul's best guess was that Esther would die within the hour.

Although we knew that this might be God's best for Esther, we were very concerned that Chris and Polly should be able to say goodbye to her before the end. We asked if he could delay disconnection until Chris and Polly arrived. To our great relief, he agreed. When the doctor and nurse left the room, we prayed together. We prayed for Chris and Polly's safety on the roads and that Esther would be spared until they arrived. The motorway had been closed earlier in the day because of snow and ice, and the weather was foul. It was a crazy thought but we both had the same thing going through our minds. With our son driving along icy motorways and Esther approaching the end, we said, "Lord, You can take one child if it's Your will but please, not both!" Agnes took words out of John's gospel to pray on our behalf. "Jesus," she said, "You are the resurrection and the life." And the truth of those words was burned more intensely on our minds to help us face what was to come.

Bombshell

To our surprise Esther's heart rate reduced and her condition became more stable. Her nurse rustled up bed linen for us so we could snatch some sleep on the chairs in the relatives' room. Sleep didn't come easily and we had just dropped off when Chris and Polly arrived. It was now about 6.00am. What an enormous relief it was to see them! But as we explained what the medical team had said to us, their distress began to show.

As we gathered as a family at her bedside, Esther appeared peaceful. We gently stroked her hands and forehead. The ventilator had been removed and she was breathing on her own. But the monitors told us her heart rate was unsustainably fast.

Chris prayed for her healing and we were very moved by the faith his persistent praying showed. Here was a young man taking Jesus' words at their face value and claiming His power in his sister's life. Here was urgent, believing prayer in action and it thrilled our hearts to hear him praying so earnestly. But healing? It didn't resonate with us, possibly because we had already started to come to terms with the inevitable and had begun to receive God's peace about it.

There was no response, so we went to find some breakfast. That may sound callous in the circumstances but we found our minds oscillating between the intensely emotional and the mundanely practical, with each feeding the other. The medical team assured us that we'd get a call if there was any change, so back at the guesthouse we tucked into bacon, eggs and oatcakes as dawn broke.

Chris and Polly became very upset. Understandably, Chris felt that we should be praying more for Esther's healing, in line with Scripture. We explained that we had complete confidence that God was capable of healing her but we weren't convinced He wanted us to pray for complete recovery. Ian's picture had given us a sense of peace that God was in command of the situation, even though it was harrowing for us. The realisation that Esther was not going to recover was now dawning on Chris and Polly, as it had earlier dawned on us.

Back in the hospital, we had a precious time when we were all able to tell Esther how much she had meant to us. Ian read from the Bible, inserting her name:

> Jesus said, "Do not let your hearts be troubled. Trust in God; trust also in me. In my Father's house are many rooms; if it were not so, I would have told you. I am going there to prepare a place for you, *Esther Mary White*. And if I go and prepare a place for you, I *will* come back and take you to be with me that you also may be where I am." (John 14:1-4)

As her condition remained stable, Chris realised how resilient his sister was. Recalling her exceptional physical stamina, he joked, "A girl who trots up a hill with an 18 kilo rucksack on her back isn't going to give up easily!" It was a moment of light relief while it felt as if time was standing still. But we could see the strain on Chris's face.

Rosi

I left the room for a while and found myself asking the Lord to take her sooner rather than later. Was that prayer for my comfort, or for hers, or for Chris's? It's hard to tell. When I returned to the ward, her breathing was laboured and less regular. Her head was flopped to one side and her fingertips were beginning to turn blue.

Bombshell

Ian

So this is what death looks like.

The person we had seen grow, mature, run, laugh, cry and bring such joy, now lay in a bed, her life ebbing away with her head resting on my arm. By God's grace we were all there when she took her last breath. It happened almost imperceptibly. There was one breath and the next simply didn't come. I looked at the attending nurse and whispered, "I think it's all over." But to my surprise she shook her head, pointing to the monitor. The heart that had been so strong through our daughter's life was still beating. Weakly, but it was still beating. We gazed at the monitor and, as we held her hand, we watched the trace gradually sink to a thin continuous line. There was no high-pitched bleep that you see in the movies, no crash team barging in to revive her, just some hospital staff and a grief-wrenched family standing in quiet reverence, as their loved one slipped out of this life, her head still on my arm.

Ian and Rosi

It was a profound and peaceful moment. We were instinctively aware that Esther's spirit had left her failed body. Ian asked for a lock of her hair to take as a keepsake and her nurse agreed to cut it when they had removed all the tubes. We felt we needed to keep something of her, something tangible, something physical, something that was actually a part of her.

Esther died at 1.45pm on Wednesday 11th February 2009. We were ushered to another part of the ward while the nurses prepared her body. Our heads told us that we wouldn't see her alive ever again, but our hearts couldn't grasp the magnitude of what had just happened. It was some minutes later that we were called to say our final goodbyes. She looked very different. Her body was still warm but her skin colour was changing to a grey pallor. Her plaited hair with its girlish white ribbon bow was still lying across the pillow.

Ian

It was my final act of love, the only way I could think a grieving father could honour the daughter he so loved and admired. Standing in awe of her body that had now finished its purpose, I leaned over and gave her a single kiss on her forehead.

"Goodbye darling," I whispered.

And together we left the room.

2

Roller-coaster

Ian and Rosi

T he mobile phone warbled into life. "I'm sorry I need to ask you about this now," said the nurse, "but we would like to talk to you about organ donation."

Although we understood the need to settle this as soon as possible after someone dies, the question came from out of the blue. In the numbness and disbelief at losing our child, the decision of what happened to her body parts was the last thing on our minds. Was this a surgical intrusion into the sanctity of her body or a comforting opportunity for someone else to benefit from her life? We were in no state to decide in that moment. We both felt assured that her spirit had left her body and was now somewhere far better, but slicing out parts of it seemed to be an invasion of her physical frame which was still very precious to us. Then looking at it another way, in character Esther was generous and self-giving to a fault. We could imagine that, given the option, she would be pleased that someone else was using parts of a body she no longer needed.

In the event, this became oddly positive. None of us had ever talked with her about whether someone else could benefit from her body when she no longer needed it, but we instinctively knew that she would want others to gain from whatever she could offer – even in death. It took a conscious decision to adopt the attitude of willingness for her body to be used for others.

"Someone will be in touch with you," said the nurse.

Breaking the news

Ian and Rosi

The task of telling people now began. We wanted our close friends, family and colleagues to receive personal phone calls from us so they didn't hear it along the grapevine. But this had a consequence neither of us anticipated. We found the constant repetition of our story quickly became wearing. Phone call after phone call had us spilling out the story all over again to different people. After a dozen or so calls, we realised we were trying to tell it in different ways for different people and that the constant reinvention of the text was scratching at raw emotions with every call.

"Can we make this easier on ourselves?" we mused. "For Mark we're spinning the student part of the story, for Liz we're trying to talk about God's plan and for Anna we're talking about possible arrangements. We're making up a new version for each person – and we're wearing ourselves down."

So we decided on a few phrases and sentences we could use with everyone we phoned. It was not that we felt we wanted to tell everyone exactly the same message for fear of getting it wrong. Much more, we found repeating a message we'd prepared in advance made it a little less painful when we had to say it over and over again.

By doing this, we found ourselves detaching our emotions from the message enough to make the sharing of it manageable. This simple method eased the pressure. We also began to listen. To listen as carefully as our emotions would allow to what friends were saying to us when we called. We had expected people to say how sorry they were but the outpouring of love and concern we heard, even over the phone, moved us profoundly. In a wonderful way it began to form the foundation of comfort that we would draw on so deeply in the weeks that followed.

Back at the hotel, we were touched by the owner's kindness. His establishment was full that night but he negotiated a discounted price for Chris and Polly in another hotel nearby. It seemed as if our plight drew compassion from people around us, even though we were virtual strangers. And it wasn't just him. Peter, a close friend from Eastbourne, was travelling to the north of England on business and rang us to ask if we would like him to visit. To discover that he was willing to change his flight plans to come to Glasgow for the night was very humbling. His was the first face from home we had seen since it all began.

Not long after Peter's arrival, Kit, Agnes and William Philip (the senior minister of Esther's church) came to see us. They brought a tenderness with them and let us spill out the events of the day. William then asked us if we had thought about commemoration services. It might seem insensitive to be thinking about funeral arrangements so soon after Esther's death, but talking about practicalities felt less demanding than constantly going over what had just happened. It gave us a focus, something to latch on to, something that diverted our minds a little.

Our proposal of a cremation in Scotland followed by a service in Eastbourne was greeted with some surprise. There was a feeling of wanting to get it over with quickly, and in retrospect we can see this emotion was clouding our judgement.

"Esther had been very unwell in her room," William said. "It's awfully smelly and I don't suggest you go there just yet. We have some people in the church who will go and clear it up, if you'd like them to."

In his gentle but firm Scots brogue he was trying to save us from further pain. Seeing the squalor in which Esther had slipped into unconsciousness would only intensify our suffering, and here were people offering to help. This is what being part of a church is all about, and now we were on the receiving end.

William prayed for us with gentle eloquence. Here was a man who chose his words carefully as he talked to God. It was as if God was present in the room as the enormity of the truths of the Christian faith came home to us again. We weren't able to pray much. A few trite phrases perhaps, but William voiced what we wanted to say with the depth of experience of a caring pastor. We felt God there. We felt held by the care and prayers of people who hardly knew us, but who cared because they had known Esther.

What do you do the evening after your daughter has just died? Everything seems abnormal. We were too numbed to feel much and in a strange way carried on as normal, although we were running on autopilot.

Autopilot led us into a Thai restaurant. It sat behind a dowdy Glasgow shopfront in a terrace of dowdy Glasgow shopfronts. The instant we opened the door, a diminutive waitress greeted us like distant relatives. "It's *so* good to see you! So good! You can sit anywhere! Come! Sit here!" She pointed us to what may have been her favourite table.

"Drinks. Can I please take order for drinks?" she said, her staccato tone punctuating the relative silence.

"Yes, but hold on a second," Ian replied as we settled into our seats.

She stood, her eyes darting around the room as if she still needed to notch up every detail. The order was fairly simple but she wrote furiously on a memo pad no bigger than a postage stamp. Moments later there was a shuffling sound as she returned, putting water, glasses and a bottle of wine on the table with a loud plonk.

"Good. This is good!" she said, as she arranged the glasses and scurried around getting cutlery in the right position on each place setting. Her next salvo came instantly.

"Food. Can I take order for food?"

"Not yet, thanks. Give us a couple of minutes."

"Two minutes. OK, I come back in two minutes."

One hundred and twenty seconds later she was back, the rapid staccato footfall from beneath her ankle length tubular dress alerting us to her arrival.

"Food. Can I take order for food now?"

"Sorry, not yet, thanks. Give us another couple of minutes."

"Two minutes. OK, I come back in two minutes."

The same pattern repeated itself at intervals over the next forty minutes as the food was served and eaten. This waitress provided non-stop entertainment as she scuttled backwards and forwards, asking if we had what we expected, picking up dropped forks and taking away any empty plate the instant it had fallen into disuse. She provided a hilarious diversion from grieving.

Thursday

Rosi

"Happy birthday, darling!" It was Ian's voice that came to me first as we woke in bed that morning. I had completely overlooked that it was my birthday until that moment. Celebrating was the furthest thing from my mind as the numbness of the previous day returned.

It soon became a busy morning with more phone calls. The police wanted to investigate the circumstances surrounding Esther's death. Then the whole issue of tissue donation began in earnest. Ian had several long conversations with the organ donation department, who asked for large amounts of detailed information about Esther's movements round the world, her illnesses, her lifestyle and her sexuality. As we talked, we began to hope that her organs would be useful to other people somewhere in the country, but the tone of the conversation changed when he mentioned Bolivia.

"Where exactly was she in Bolivia?"

"She began in La Paz and then went to a church in a more rural location. I'm sorry, I don't remember the name of the place off-hand."

There was a pause.

"I'm sorry," came the reply. "Rural Bolivia is off-limits. There is an obscure virus which hides itself in the bloodstream and may not affect the sufferer until years after they come back home. We have no way of knowing whether or not Esther was infected with it, but it means we can't take the risk of using her organs. There is an outside chance someone in the UK could be infected by it if she was a carrier. Incidentally, were you aware that Esther was on the organ donation register?"

"Completely unaware."

"It would still be possible for us to use her corneas, though. Would you be willing for that to happen?"

"Of course."

Having been initially taken aback by the talk of donating, we were now curiously disappointed that no more of her body could be used. But we have the comfort of knowing that someone, somewhere, is now seeing the world through Esther's eyes.

One of the consequences of being church leaders is the congregation of people we needed to talk to – our church family as well as our blood relatives. This is not the sort of news you can trust to the grapevine so we began the task of deciding what should be said to them. It was important to us that we communicated well, balancing our own sadness with the hope of the Christian message. Ian and I had both written down a few ideas about the statement to be read out to the church when they next met on the Sunday morning. We did this independently, but significantly our ideas were very similar, and even the words and phrases we were using married up. Within a couple of hours we had agreed on how to convey it, and sent it off.

Invading Esther's privacy

Ian

Esther had always maintained a very private side to her personality. There were parts of her life into which, as parents, we had learned not to probe. So sorting through her belongings so soon after she'd died felt like an intrusion into her private arena, and yet it was a practical necessity.

The Road Not Chosen

This meant a visit to her house. I did not relish the prospect of going there. This was Esther's domain and a place I had not visited while she was alive. To go through her front door was to intrude in part of her life into which I had not been invited. This was her space, her sphere, and would evoke all the memories of who she had been. At the same time I was intrigued to see her world and to try to glean something about her final months from the people who lived with her. Maybe the house itself had a story to tell. I had heard about the piano, but never played it. I had heard about the living-room, but never sat on the sofa.

Climbing the winding stairs leading to her room felt like making a pilgrimage to a hallowed place. The door which had hidden her as she slipped into unconsciousness swung open and I was accosted by a heady mix of pine disinfectant and vanilla air freshener. Tucked into a gable in the roof, the room had an unusual geometry. Parts of the ceiling slanted down at offbeat angles and the desk obscured the lower part of the only window. A chair was squeezed in next to the desk and a stool doubled as a bedside table. I stood there taking in the scene that had been my daughter's living space. Files leaned against each other on the shelf as if needing mutual support. Notes and diagrams littered the desk, the chair and the floor. Clothes were draped randomly. So this was how she lived and how she died. I went to sit on her bed but only bare boards remained.

"We took away the mattress," said Kit. "It was pretty mucky."

He didn't know it, but those four words made my heart lurch. They drove home to me the harrowing nature of her final hours in this oddly shaped room. Someone had cleaned up the residue of Esther's vomit and masked it with vanilla. That anonymous act of kindness filled me with gratitude but the tang of sick still hung in the air.

Roller-coaster

Ian and Rosi

Sorting through her possessions was never going to be easy. Here, in these scattered objects, was Esther's life, her work, her clothes and all her treasured bric-a-brac. Likely as not, things she would have wanted to conceal from us were about to be laid bare. Every piece of paper, every unmatched sock, every journal entry and even her prized collection of Marmite jars had to be decided upon. On the desk lay an intricate drawing of an elbow and in a corner lurked a fibreglass foot. The occasional life-sized model of a body part only added to the surreal nature of sorting through her possessions.

For her degree, Esther had been studying Prosthetics and Orthotics, and she had never considered any other option. A television programme she watched in her mid-teens had been a life-changing turning point. The documentary maker had shown the impact a simple prosthetic can make in the life of an amputee. Landmines, motorcycle accidents and congenital deformity all contribute to this particular tide of human misery, and Esther believed she could make a difference. It was as if a light turned on in her heart, and from that moment on she was going to live out her Christian faith by giving people limbs and helping them to walk.

As we sifted through the contents of her room, there were moments when we all wept. Even a casual glance through her journals showed us the depth of her walk with God, juxtaposed with the intensity of her struggles with life. She was so doggedly determined to achieve her goals and overcome her difficulties that we were moved to tears. One of the posters she had made for herself spoke as if she was her own life coach: "At the end of your life I want you to look back and remember that YOU held nothing back, YOU did not lose heart, YOU did not stop fighting, YOU did not quit."[1]

---

[1]   It is reproduced on the cover, complete with its original grease mark.

The Road Not Chosen

Such tenacity we still find humbling.

"Esther just didn't know how to quit," said Chris.

Moments later, in the next room into which some of her belongings had overflowed, Chris found brand new Ordnance Survey maps of the Scottish West Highlands. He came to us, holding them out like trophies, his eyes rimmed with tears.

"Look at these," he said. "My last conversation with her had been to ask her if she'd like to walk the West Highland Way with me ... and she'd said yes. Look, she'd even bought the maps! In fact she was so keen, she was going to ask Christine to join us. I was waiting for Esther to get back to me."

We found moments like these, and there were many of them, both harrowing and healing. Our minds have an enormous capacity for recollection, even of the tiniest things, when they are stimulated by objects, papers and smells. We didn't realise it at the time but riding the emotional roller-coaster helped to put things in place. It helped to sort out the important from the trivial and began to frame the memories we would draw on in the future. We knew we had a time pressure to complete some of this work, but had we left it, we would probably have carried wounds that would have been more difficult to heal as time passed.

Two hours later we had finished. But nagging at the back of our minds was a question. Had we kept the right things? Had we kept the stuff that Esther valued, or just those things that intrigued us? In fact the question of how much we should keep dominated our minds. We only had a suitcase in which to carry anything back to Eastbourne. The idea of coming to Glasgow to see our daughter in hospital, hopefully to nurse her back to health, but returning with a borrowed suitcase full of her remaining possessions, filled us with anguish.

Zoe and Christine, who also shared the house with Esther, arrived with Agnes. We felt some awkwardness as they clearly felt they should be comforting us, but in the event we found ourselves reassuring them. In all of our minds there was bewilderment over how Esther could have been in her room, slipping into a coma while nobody noticed. We all needed to piece together the sequence of events to understand a little more about how it had happened. It was not an easy meeting. There were far too many "If only" statements. "If only I had done this ..." or "If only I had said that ..." things might have turned out so differently.

Zoe, for example, said she had seen Esther on Saturday afternoon, thought she looked sleepy and suspected she had not done her morning shift at the nursing home. Esther had asked where Christine was, which Christine herself thought was strange as Esther had known that she was flying to her uncle's funeral. It made us realise that she might already have been confused and showing signs of being very unwell.

This was not the first time Christine had expressed concern to us over Esther. She observed how much quieter and introverted Esther had become since they were friends in Eastbourne. She wondered what Esther was going to do at the end of the year as she seemed to have no prospects or plans. Working in the nursing home and completing her degree might have been too much for her. When Polly had spoken to Esther about her future, the idea of not completing her course was an option she would not consider, but they both could see it was a tall order.

At this point we had a surprise. Christine revealed that Esther had confided to her that she had a "big decision" to make but had refused be drawn on what it might be. She had even written this in a Facebook entry which mystified some of her online friends. So what was this decision? Breaking her course? We will never know. Living with uncertainties like this has become a part of grieving which has always been tough to handle.

Understandably, Zoe felt guilty that there had been several people in the house but no-one had known that Esther was upstairs semi-conscious. However it was common for Zoe not to bump into her for a couple of days at a time so she had thought no more of it.

We both realised just how much Esther's friends had assumed responsibility for some of the events leading up to her being found in her room. But their sense of culpability was unfounded. Neither of us wanted them to carry a burden of guilt onward into their lives, so we were most anxious to reassure them. We didn't hold them responsible and, despite the unanswered questions, we still felt that God had His hand on her life right up to the end. Ian shared his heart with them. We only later discovered that this time became a source of help and reassurance to Esther's close friends.

Ian

The afternoon began with a visit to a local funeral director. As a minister, I often negotiate with undertakers about funerals and have become accustomed to their work behind the scenes. But being on the receiving end of their professional service was something I had rarely experienced. There was something almost surreal about being shown into a room and sat down on an uncomfortable studded red leather sofa to talk about our daughter's funeral.

The black-clad woman on duty brandished a heavy clipboard and, after a brief introduction, bombarded us with questions. Sitting behind an imposing mahogany desk on the opposite side of the room, she occasionally condescended to make eye contact with us. Her "empathy" had a mechanistic detachment to it that made me wonder if she had the slightest idea of what we might be going through. We explained our circumstances.

"We are obviously going to need to bring Esther's body back home to Eastbourne, so can you give us some advice about the process?" I asked.

She thought for a moment. "I'll have to talk to my line manager about this," she responded, and promptly left the room.

Several minutes passed before she re-emerged to say that it was possible for the trip to be arranged, and came up with a convoluted plan involving undertakers meeting halfway up the M1. I was not convinced, and said so. In my mind's eye, I could visualise these two hearses arranging to meet at some obscure service station, only to discover they couldn't cross the motorway with a coffin!

"I just need to check on something here," she said. "I'll need to see my line manager again." And with that she turned her back and left the room once more. When she returned she looked intently into her notepad and spoke to it.

"Because Esther died in Scotland and the funeral will be in England, I'm afraid this will be regarded as an international repatriation. We could arrange to fly her down."

I couldn't believe my ears. What on earth would Esther need for this journey – a new passport?

"Can you give us some idea how much all this is going to cost?" I asked. Her eyes were still fixed on the notepad.

"I can assure you that you'll definitely receive only a single bill with all the items on it," she said.

The fact that there would only be one bill seemed to be of huge importance to her. It is apparently very complicated to produce a single bill, and it seemed I ought to be grateful for her well-honed expertise in adding up the figures! Frankly I couldn't give a toss how many bills I got, so long as I knew roughly how much money I'd have to find. But when I asked what sort of figures we might be talking about, she requested another adjournment.

"I'll have to talk to my line manager about this," she responded.

Another wait.

If you're not familiar with the art of the undertaker you need to know that coffins come in all shapes and sizes. From the prestigious brass-handled hardwood monsters through to painted fibreglass with Bugs Bunny emblazoned on the sides, almost every taste can be catered for. A year previously I had taken a woodland funeral for a lady whose body had been placed in one of these wickerwork caskets. During one of her adjournments, Rosi and I had chatted about this, so I enquired if this might be possible for Esther. We felt it would look more delicately feminine and would move away from the rigid boxed-in shape of a traditional coffin.

"I'm sorry," she said, "but I don't have any pictures of those for you to look at." In fact she didn't have any catalogues or pictures at all. "I'll have to consult my line manager."

It was becoming a mantra and by this time I was getting exasperated. I eyeballed her.

"Now listen to me darling. Can't you even go to the toilet without consulting your line manager? If you can't find out basic stuff like what a coffin looks like without talking to him, why can't I speak to him myself? He's obviously somewhere here. So will you please take me to your leader. Now." I thought it, rehearsed it in my head, but mercifully bit my tongue and remained silent. But it was a close call.

Roller-coaster

Esther's body was eventually brought back to Eastbourne using two hearses who met up to transfer her from one vehicle to the other. The saving grace was that an Eastbourne undertaker I knew well was part of the same company chain. Only the previous week I had worked with her on a funeral and I was confident she would handle it sensitively – and at least she'd know what coffins looked like.

Rosi

The evening was light relief in comparison. An Italian meal and a comedy film later were like an oasis, although we did wonder whether we should be having so much fun when dealing with such weighty stuff. But the fun was a release and the unanimous verdict was, "Esther wouldn't have wanted us to be overwhelmed." Being together as a family, albeit with one missing, had a strangely reassuring feel to it.

Friday

Rosi

Having to decide whether to have a cremation or a burial for one of your children is something one never expects to do. We had no idea about Esther's views and we had gone to bed on Thursday night with sharply differing opinions. Ian was quite strongly in favour of burial and I felt otherwise. At times when we have seen things differently, we have often committed the matter to God in prayer and then shelved it for a while. We prayed that evening that we would settle the decision amicably. On Ian's part, he felt that having a place to go to visit Esther's body was very important; that there is something sacrosanct about the place where someone's remains are laid that helps relatives thank God for them. On my part I really didn't like the idea of her being confined to a box in the ground. There was something visceral about my feelings regarding this confinement. I wanted her to be free.

On Friday morning I woke with a photograph on my mind. It was a picture that Ian had taken of Esther as a teenager running into the mist on the South Downs. It came vividly to my imagination. I remembered that we had commented to each other that she seemed happy and carefree, with her long brown hair flowing behind in the breeze. When I shared this with Ian, he surprised me with his reaction. He too remembered the picture well and had never told me the impact it had on him at the time. The image of her running away from the viewer evoked in him a sense of foreboding. He felt as if Esther was running into an uncertain future, possibly even into eternity. It was probably the only time a picture had had such a strong spiritual and emotional impact on him. He had withheld telling me about this because he didn't want to appear morbid when interpreting what, in all other respects, was a simple photograph of our daughter.[1] He probably didn't want to show beyond doubt that he is the Eeyore in our relationship!

One of the things that had brought me such great delight was walking on the Downs with Esther. She found freedom on the hills as we walked and talked together, sharing those moments that only mothers and daughters can experience.

The idea of confining her to a box didn't feel right. Scattering her ashes on the Downs felt like releasing her and also would give us a delightful place we could later visit to remember her. Ian had not seen it like this before, and the more we talked about it together, the more we felt that this was the best way to honour Esther.

---

[1] It's the image on the cover art of this book.

Roller-coaster

Ian and Rosi

Chris seemed anxious to return home, and we were aware of the mounting toll the events of the past two days had taken on him. Parting in circumstances like these was tough, yet we all knew that at some point we would have to pick up the reins of life again, even while we had so much planning to do. We always felt that the strong love and support we had for each other would see us through this toughest of times. It had already seen us through lesser life challenges. Facing the smaller difficulties with God at our side helped to prepare us for the weightier things that are almost inevitable.

We too needed to check out of the hotel as they were full that evening, but there was still much to do. Registering Esther's death, it turned out, was not going to be as straightforward as we'd hoped. Being an unexpected death, the police were involved and clearance to register couldn't be given until the Procurator Fiscal had put his signature on the right piece of paper. The church let us base ourselves in a spare office from which we organised the funeral. Their kindness was exceptional. Tea, coffee and sandwiches seemed to appear at just the right moments, and some of the staff who knew Esther came in to tell us moving stories about how she had contributed to their children's holiday club in the Isle of Skye. Her quirky sense of humour had not been lost on them either. So far as Esther's church, St George's Tron, was concerned, Ian wasn't the minister and therefore was on the receiving end of their pastoral concern. So our relationships with the people in the church did not contain the complicating factor of being their pastor.

By mid-afternoon we were in a position to collect Esther's death certificate, which needed to be delivered to a registrar. So far, so good. But as we once again sat in the side room of the ITU waiting to be called, we could see the minutes ticking past and tension within us began to mount. The certificate needed to be with the registrar at 4.30 and he was a train journey away. The other relatives who also sat in the waiting room were burdened people, just like us, and we wondered about their stories. When we eventually got to see the doctor, he took his time to explain all that had happened. In our naïvety we thought he would have seen situations like this before but he admitted, "This has really shaken us. There are questions we've got to ask about why someone so young and so fit could die so quickly from diabetes."

It was in moments like this that we began to ask some of the obvious, but awkward, questions that were to prey on our minds for months to come. Exactly why did Esther die? Could we have done anything to save her? Were any of the medics culpable? She had come into hospital as a serious but straightforward case of hypoglycaemia[1] and yet she'd lost her life. Why – oh why?

With the death certificate in our hands we made a dash for the registrar, knowing we had to be there by 4.30. Dragging heavy suitcases, one with our belongings, the other with Esther's, we clattered through the streets of Glasgow and arrived, panting, two minutes before the deadline. Curiously we were faced with an office building that was firmly locked. Ringing the bell had no effect and after a few moments a weary-looking administrator let herself out through the already activated security system.

"Any chance of delivering a death certificate?" we said.

"Sorry," came the tired response. "We closed half an hour ago."

---

[1]   Hypoglycaemia is an abnormally low level of glucose in the blood, which leaves the body without enough energy to carry out its activities. It is most commonly associated with diabetes, and mainly occurs if someone with diabetes takes too much insulin, misses a meal or exercises too hard.

Roller-coaster

Ian was livid. Not with the woman who was doing no more than going home for tea, but with the bureaucracy. We had pulled all the stops out to get this piece of paper to the right place by 4.30 and now we had to come up with another plan if we were going to get to Glasgow Airport in time for our flight. We returned dejectedly to the Tron, and once again Agnes went out of her way to help. She agreed to deliver the certificate to the registrar and send the papers on to us. It seemed like all our emotions were heightened and it was much more difficult to be objective.

Returning to home and to normality felt like an enormous relief. But we arrived to find the porch of our home filled with flowers. Normality had changed forever and there was still a long journey ahead.

3

Strangeness

Lonely in Ireland, since it was not home, Strangeness made sense. (Philip Larkin)

This world is not my home, I'm just a-passin thru ... and I don't feel at home in this world any more. (Negro Spiritual)

Ian

Home now had a sense of strangeness. Returning to Eastbourne, it felt odd to see life going on as if nothing had happened. Almost everything in our house directed me down a road which led to Esther. These were the stairs she climbed. These were the pots and pans she cooked with. These were the felt tips she used to create her drawings. Entering the living-room I could hear the volume of the piano's silence. This was where she learned her music and wrote her compositions, played and sang to the applause of an invisible audience. But on each of these roads there was a barrier, an obstacle I couldn't bypass: she had gone. There would be no more climbing stairs, cooking or music-making. Each road which would once have led to new discoveries was now a cul-de-sac.

This feeling was so strong that at times I seemed to be an observer watching a stage play in which I had only a bit part.

The events that had traumatised us were, to the man in the street, somebody else's story. A scene in someone else's life. So why should he care or even notice? This sense of detachment stayed with us for months.

Seeing familiar people and doing familiar things, however, gave a comforting sense of the commonplace, and although we felt raging emotional turmoil, there was a growing awareness that life could, and one day would, return to a new normality. At the same time there was an unnerving unpredictability in our emotions. It felt as if the path of grief we were now beginning was going to last forever, even though our minds and our professional experience told us otherwise.

One thing we had not expected was the tiredness – nobody told us that grieving was such exhausting work. It wasn't that we were any busier than usual – as leaders we were both quite comfortable with taking responsibility and organising events – but instead of taking them in our stride, some of the simplest things exhausted us.

Places of safety

Rosi

We found we needed places of safety where we could just be ourselves, and we came to call them our "oases". My sister Eleanor lives with her husband in leafy Surrey and we decided to visit them. Here was a place where we could talk freely and be ourselves. We were free from the pressure of expectation that church or public appearances foisted on us. We had had many offers of meals in our friends' homes back in Eastbourne, and while we knew each one was well-meaning, we also knew we would have to tell our story yet again and relive the pain of it. We weren't ready for that.

Strangeness

Somehow Eleanor and Andrew's home was safe, their company undemanding and their empathy unforced. They gave us precious space in which it was Ian and I who decided the trajectory of our conversation, and whatever words we used fell on receptive ears, there simply to listen. We are not a particularly huggy family but when I could hold back the tears no longer, Eleanor took me in her arms and held me so I could weep through it, without saying a word. Here I found love, compassion, mercy, sympathy and simple humanity exquisitely woven into a hug. In incremental steps, they began bringing hope for recovery. The prospect of one day being restored.

Ian

My mother, Grace, was at the stage of life where she needed the care of a residential home. She was frail, suffering with a failing memory, and plagued with anxiety. But I could see beyond her wizened features to the mother we knew in times past. She had brought an effervescent enthusiasm to our childhood home that was grounded with savvy wisdom and touched the lives of people who crossed our doorstep. She was Grace by name and grace by nature. The staff of the residential home, who with Job-like patience catered for her needs, were concerned that such disquieting news would agitate her further. My brother Carey had already told her that Esther had passed away but we felt we should go as soon as possible to reassure her and to share her sadness, as best we could.

Such was the unpredictability of her memory that we could not be sure whether she would recall the news Carey had brought, or whether it would have slithered out of her failing mind. This made me approach our chat with some trepidation. If she had remembered, she could be so burdened with the weight of it that her mind might be overwhelmed with its sadness. And if this was happening, would it be possible for her to self-restore? Alternatively she might have forgotten altogether, and I would be telling her as if it was fresh news. I couldn't decide which would be the easier to bear, forgetting or remembering. My dear Mum, who brought me into the world, who had been a constant companion and ally, whose determination and self-sacrifice paved the way for me to follow my dreams, was now a frail old lady. In the last year she had become increasingly forgetful and obsessively worried about running out of clothes. Last month she had taken my hand and looked me in the eye: "D'you know," she shared, her fervent smile paving the way for the ultimate compliment, "You do look like my son." Ageing is vicious.

There was a ritual to visiting Grace. Arrive, make sure she knew who she was talking to, and then listen to her latest collection of anxieties. This time again it was clothes. We were often asked to do a tally of her drawers. So we faithfully counted out her pants to reassure her that she had enough to get to the end of the week without what, for her, was the ultimate embarrassment.

We were soon, however, talking about Esther and sharing the events that had just taken place in Glasgow. Thankfully she had remembered. As she listened, it seemed to trigger a nascent ability to empathise and something of her old caring groundedness returned. This was another safe place to talk about all we'd experienced. We ended by praying together and making to leave the home. As we walked away, she motioned to me to come back. The look on her face suggested she had remembered something important she wanted to say. As we bent down to listen, she adopted a tone of great gravity and said (in a single breath):

"Ian, I'm *so* sorry about your loss ... and I'm *so* worried about my pants."

It was as much as we could do not to collapse in hysterics. The juxtaposition of such extreme opposites tickled us both. But it was curiously reassuring. At least she had remembered that

Esther had gone and at the same time it wasn't dominating her mental landscape.

And we still had knickers to count.

Kindness

Ian and Rosi

Back in Eastbourne, the doorbell rang. Standing there with a heavy object under a towel stood one of the young mums in the church. Life was a struggle for her with two young children and a low income. Before we could even say hello, she blurted out, "I just didn't know what to do, so I made you dinner," and handed us a steaming sausage casserole. Plenty of carbs here, then! What moved us most was not the cuisine but the enormous love that was packed into that meal. This mum had spent precious time to create something that spoke of her love for us, at a time when we needed it most.

And it wasn't only meals. Friends came round to do nothing else but to listen and give us one of the most precious gifts we received: time. Unforced time, uncritical time, and sometimes a long time.

The prospect of being separated from each other was still unnerving for both of us, although we knew it had to happen. Ian's appointment with his GP was likely to be the first time we had been apart since we'd returned from Glasgow. Then just as Ian was leaving the house, two people came to the door. Jo and Susie were the kind of people we found it easy to confide in. They were leaders of a different local church, and we had become friends, sharing our hearts with them over numerous meals. This was a remarkable piece of God's timing, not only because Rosi had some company but also because she was beginning to find the whole repetition of the tragedy stressful.

During the weeks that followed we had invitation after invitation to outings and meals with friends and acquaintances – far more than we could possibly accept. Every one was an act of kindness which we found ourselves appreciating more and more. Our emotions, however, were still raw and sometimes we found it hard to reconcile our friends' joviality with our sadness.

Ian

There was sometimes an assumption that, as a grieving couple, what we really needed was to be cheered up. The unsaid message was that sadness was inappropriate for Christians, especially Christian leaders, and that we needed this fixed. This is an assumption that still needs to be challenged, as what we needed in those moments was uncritical listening, not jollity. Other people set themselves up as armchair experts on grieving and saw us as people in dire need of their expertise. What we needed was empathy, not information; we needed love, not advice. And while I'm convinced every one of the people we encountered in this time was well-meaning, it made us write a note to self: handle grieving people with empathy!

The office

Rosi

The phone rang; it was my boss.

"Ros," (they never called me Rosi) "we're all devastated to hear about your daughter. We had no idea it was so serious and we're all really sorry."

Strangeness

Once again I used our chosen sentences to share the events with her. It moved me to hear how upset my work colleagues had been about the death of someone they had never met.

"Is there anything we can ... do?" she asked.

That's a natural enough question to ask but a difficult one for grieving people to answer. It was as if my team wanted to take some practical action to make both them and us feel better about it all. But practical things are hard to think of when most of the ordinary stuff of life is taken care of. At that moment I had a brainwave – more of a whim, really. Maybe meeting face to face might help all of us as we grappled with what had happened. I made the suggestion.

"Ros, you can't believe how relieved I am! We'll put it together for Thursday lunchtime. Is that OK? Are you sure you can cope with this?"

Relief? Now that I didn't expect. Maybe it was relief that their sorrow was not purposeless and we could at least face it together in some small way.

When the time came, Ian and I were greeted by an unexpectedly large group. The only available space turned out to be a seminar room. As we entered, the fragrance of fresh polish wafted through the air and the U-shape arrangement of the tables, the NOBO flip chart and multicoloured felt tips gave it the air of a lecture room. But standing out as if unfamiliar with its surroundings was a tea set that wouldn't have been out of place in a stately home. From somewhere, someone had brought out the best bone china they could find and, in our honour, had put at its centre an enormous chocolate sponge cake.

I have no idea where all this came from, and I never saw it again, but it was a lovely touch. We drank the coffee, chatting as it went down, and then there was a surreal silence. Now that we were together, no-one quite knew where to take it. So, a little unsure of ourselves, we began to share our story, starting with Ian preaching on the Sunday and my gift of a book about heaven. As we retold the events, empathy flowed through their attentive smiles. Listening is such a powerful act.

Ian

As I was talking, I became aware of puzzled faces. Some people were a little bemused by the spiritual component of the events. I was very aware that, in contrast to a Sunday congregation, I was talking with people who probably didn't have any concept of God-ordained strength or a divine purpose in tragedy. It felt as if they were having difficulty grasping the spiritual angle of all we were telling them, especially God's coincidences and the way they meshed together in His plan for us. I found myself saying, "If we weren't Christians this would all sound really spooky," and I saw gentle nods of agreement. This was another privileged moment where Esther's death was being used by her heavenly Father to speak of how knowing Christ really makes a difference.

"If being a Christian doesn't work now," I found myself saying, "it doesn't work, period."

The local press

Ian

We'd had a call from a local newspaper reporter. I was never quite sure how they got wind of Esther's death but, although tactful, she clearly wanted the story. I feared she might take our story and twist it into a journalistic scoop, headlined "tragedy", "anger" or "shock-horror". However the reality was very different. She was empathetic, concerned both to get the facts right and also to attach our preferred interpretation to them. On her own admission, she was struck by our desire to allow our experience to make us better people, not bitter people. "I'm going to write that down," she said, and dutifully entered it in her notebook.

Rosi

I don't know what it is about us, but the conversation soon changed, with the reporter telling us about her own father's death. She shared openly about how she'd struggled, before eventually coming to terms with it. Was this going to be the shape of things to come? Would God use our experience to draw out others' tragedy and help them talk about it? We felt our story was giving us a strange sort of celebrity status we had never looked for. The reporter left to compose her article and Ian gave her his best photo of Esther for publication.

A few days later, the phone rang again.

"Ros, I need to have a word with you." The voice came from a neighbour and was laden with concern. "Just been to the newsagent and seen something I don't like. You're on all the posters! 'Tragedy of student's death' is being plastered all over the hoardings." It seems we had become headline news and Esther's story was in huge letters on the A-frames. Thinking we didn't know about the newspaper article, our neighbour had asked the shop owner to put it away because we only lived round the corner.

Ian

On my doormat dropped two letters from my doctor on the same day. My recent blood test results had arrived and I was being called to the surgery to discuss them. This was most unusual. Normally I'm told, "Ring us in a week and we'll tell you the results over the phone." But this letter had the air of a summons. More worryingly still was that, among the clutch of tests, one was for diabetes and my GP wanted "one of the tests to be repeated". Once again my mind went into overdrive. Could it be that the very condition that had just taken Esther to eternity was now affecting me? At the time Esther was diagnosed, I had agonised in prayer, "Lord, I'm willing to carry this condition if You'll take it from her. I've had a good life and she has yet to have the adventure. Lord, she doesn't deserve this. Esther with diabetes seems so unfair!" Could this transfer of her condition to me now be taking place, and if so why hadn't it taken place in her lifetime to spare her the pain? While she was alive, I would happily have traded places with her if it had been possible, but not now. What on earth was the point?

"OK, God," I raged in frustration. "What does this say about You, then? Are You teaching me some kind of lesson? Am I being punished? And what does that make You, then? A loving Sovereign to be trusted or a quirky deity to be appeased?" In retrospect I can see the craziness of praying like this but we don't think or pray rationally when we're grieving. However I believe that God is insightful enough to see through rage and stick with us in the raging. I knew that in the Bible there were examples of people who complained to God bitterly and still came to a place of trusting Him.[1] I still had some way to go.

I arranged an appointment in a hurry and my head was in a spin as I entered the waiting room. There, with the noticeboards crammed with amateurishly printed medical announcements and a table stacked with out-of-date editions

---

[1] King David in Psalm 22 is a good example. He felt totally abandoned by God and didn't mince his words. He eventually came to a place where he discovered God in a fresh way, but there is no indication this was a quick process.

of *Country Life*, my mind was filled with foreboding. After ruminating in a plastic chair for what seemed like an hour, my name was called. There were the usual routine pleasantries and my GP nonchalantly went through the stats. At any moment I was expecting his tone to change with the message "I'm afraid I've got bad news about your blood sugar levels" but it never did. Instead he was telling me everything seemed normal and he finished with, "... the good news is you only have a 9% chance of a heart attack in the next ten years. Hey, pull up your chair and just look at this!" I moved so I could see his screen and he proudly showed off his new piece of software that was making this uncanny prediction. "Ian, that means you've got a 91% chance of avoiding one!"

There was not a word about diabetes.

Planning

Ian

It was still only seven days after Esther's death but by this time the church in Eastbourne needed to know the details of an order of service for her funeral. There was also talk about having another service in Glasgow for her friends and university staff who would not be able to fly to the south coast. Until this moment I just hadn't been capable of giving any of this much serious thought and I found myself struggling with the conflict between the professional and the personal. I felt it was sad, even unfair, that I had no-one to sit alongside me to do what I do so often for other grieving families. I didn't feel anyone was to blame for this but this quirk of my position highlighted the peculiar loneliness of leadership. My mind couldn't think straight and I was uncharacteristically finding planning confusing.

The Road Not Chosen

Rosi

We needed to find another oasis. It came in the form of a meal with our son Chris and his wife Polly. Sharing our experiences and allowing each other to be silent was drawing us closer to each other. It was over the meal that they did "the big reveal." They had bought tickets for a piano concert. For our birthdays. Ian's passion for piano music and my enjoyment of concerts combined to make it a significant oasis. But something hit me during that meal – our family was now smaller. Never again would there be the five of us sharing our banter over special food. It was a curious mixture of the hilarious and the hurtful.

It would have been easy for me to feel guilty about enjoyment as if sadness needed to dominate my life out of respect for Esther. Ian and I found moments of distraction and pleasure were a welcome break from the burden of planning funerals and coming to terms with Esther's absence. There would be plenty of time for us to meet these demands.

We spent the next day planning. We were now looking towards four events: a committal at a crematorium, a thanksgiving service in Eastbourne, another in Glasgow and a meal for our extended family. Organising four events simultaneously gave us projects to focus on. However the stress sometimes bubbled to the surface and the sparks flew between Ian and me. There seemed to be so much to do and although our friends were anxious to help us, it was beginning to feel like a huge burden.

Ian

Somehow we had tried to convince ourselves that we could manage, but we now knew we would have to swallow our pride and ask for much more help than we thought we'd need. My PA and the church administrator were exceptionally supportive and reassured us that it was a pleasure, even a privilege, to do additional work for us. My default position as the church's primary leader is to assume I can cope, but at this moment any claim to personal strength was a thin veneer. Asking for so much help on a personal matter to do with my own family didn't come naturally to me. But I learned through this that it was healing to be on the receiving end of other people's love and support when my own resources were so depleted.

Rosi

I wish I could convey to you the emotional intensity of all this. All the planning combined with constantly being sensitive to each other's feelings was exhausting. There were so many decisions to be made and each one seemed to carry an emotional weight of its own. We wanted to "get it right" in honour of Esther, but what did "right" look like anyway? We often tried to put ourselves into Esther's shoes and ask what she would have wanted, but even that added pressure to the smallest decision. Slowly we felt it coming together.

It was another oasis. A muddy walk round a local reservoir got us out of the house. When Ian and I walk together our time is usually peppered with conversation but for most of this walk we were silent, taking comfort only in each other's presence.

Ian

Many years before, when Esther was still a baby, I had adapted a Michael Perry song to be sung at her dedication service. At the time we wanted to make it clear that the Lord was to be part of our lives and we wanted to find a way of expressing this, and the idea that our children were on loan from Him. These words summed up our desire at that seminal moment:

The Road Not Chosen

Lord Jesus Christ, invited guest and Saviour,
with tender mercy hear us as we pray;
grant our desire – we come to seek your favour;
as we give Esther back to you today.

Give her your strength for caring and for serving,
give her your graces – faithfulness and prayer;
make her resolve to follow you unswerving,
make her reward your peace beyond compare.

Be her delight in joy, her hope in sorrow,
be her true friend in pleasure and in pain;
guest of today and guardian of tomorrow,
guard her young life and in our family reign.[1]

We wept as we read these words together. It seemed that the prayer expressed in every line had been answered. It was remarkable how we could identify so many God-incidences in Esther's life, as if He had a special place in His heart for her. It was as if He knew we would need these reassurances as we adapted to the end of her earthly journey. We recalled for example how God provided two other Christians for Esther to live with in her first year residence and one of them was even doing the same course. We reminisced about how her friends at school had written about Esther being a caring and generous person. We remembered how her journal showed she had called out to God in times of sorrow and, although there was another side of Esther that we were only beginning to discover, this was a moment for thanking God for the privilege of being her parents.

Music has always been an important part of my life, and was of Esther's too, although she was rarely heard performing in public. The task of planning the music for the services now

---

[1] *Lord Jesus Christ, invited guest and Saviour* by M Perry © Mrs B Perry/The Jubilate Group. www.jubilate.co.uk. Used by permission.

came into focus. We went round to a friend's house to discuss the music for the Eastbourne thanksgiving service and arrived to discover a group of people in her home praying for us – and this moved us.

I hope I didn't show it, but I was concerned about the music. For some funeral services the music is merely an incidental part of the event and consists of a collection of favourites that the person who has died is assumed to have liked. But I wanted the music to have a much higher profile. We saw the music as being integral to the message of the service. We wanted to give people an opportunity to grieve with us, but also to feel the impact of the hope of the gospel. We had chosen pieces which move the soul; pieces which can convey warmth and majesty, and I really didn't want them to be played as ditties. My friend detected my concern and asked me to play one of them at the speed I felt it should go, so I sat at her piano. Not having touched an instrument since Esther's death, I silently prayed, "Lord, give me majesty in this performance," and gave it my best shot. As the piece finished there was silence. Nobody moved.

"Oh wow!" our friend said. "I've really never heard that much sound come out of our piano before – and we've had it for twenty years!"

Gratified that she understood my musical intention, I would from now on have to trust the musicians. Having a perfectionist streak, that was never going to be easy.

Rosi

Sunday loomed like an oncoming juggernaut. At our home church in Eastbourne I expected questions to come in by the bucketload if we showed our faces. We were finding we couldn't respond to even the most well-meaning questions without feeling an urge to weep. Questions meant in love sometimes felt like interrogation. "How are you?" (Not really sure.) "What can I do to help?" (Can't think of anything right now.) "How are you coping?" (Sometimes we're not, really.) "How can we pray for you?" (We have no answer.) "Aren't you happy that Esther's in heaven?" (Not really, no.) "I'm sure God will work all things for good." (You must be joking – that's not where we are right now.) Our previous church with its close friends in Chichester felt as if it could be a haven. Here we could arrive and leave without being noticed too much and not carry the church leader mantle. Here, Esther had spent her formative years, and we felt we could worship without feeling the responsibilities of pastor and wife.

The journey passed largely in silence. Some old friends had asked us to eat with them. It was strange how, at a time like this, long-standing friends seemed reassuring. Their house, their voices, their predictable chatter created a sense of safety where we were not given a leadership or pastoral persona. Of course they had known Esther and had shared her childhood with us. "Oh yes, I remember her rabbit," our friend had said, as she mimicked the rabbit's ears. In an undefinable way, these chance remarks were comforting.

A short drive across the city brought us to the house where we once lived and where every nook and cranny oozed memories. The present incumbent was now leading this thriving church and had given us his time that afternoon. We had asked him to give the address at the Eastbourne thanksgiving service. Ken instinctively used our time together to go beyond the organisational to gently probe our own thoughts. His conversation was infused with an empathy that comes from someone who has had a few knocks of his own. We had settled on the major elements of the service but he asked if we could change the Bible reading from John 3 to Isaiah 55. Initially sceptical (and stupidly thinking this would cause complications with the printers!) we listened to his thinking. The more he opened up about how God had been speaking to him through this new passage, the more we could see it was the right one for our occasion. We left his home feeling that he had ministered to us with sensitivity and grace.

Church

Ian

I had some misgivings about attending church, any church, that Sunday. I was finding music, any music, so emotionally moving that tears were close to the surface in almost any song. This was particularly true of songs Esther might have sung when we lived in Chichester. While I managed to maintain my composure, I felt I was at risk of losing it at almost any moment. I found this really disconcerting and it helped me to understand why people I pastor sometimes avoid church when they've just been bereaved.

Another Ian, and another friend from the past, preached with passion and enthusiasm. His meticulous approach to the Bible unpacked its meaning with compelling clarity. He spoke about Jesus' praying in the garden of Gethsemane before His crucifixion (Matthew 26:36-46). In this passage Jesus appears to want to avoid the cross, but comes to a place where He can say to His heavenly Father, "Not my will but yours be done." Few words could have been more appropriate to us for that day. We would have done almost anything to have this cup of suffering lifted from us. But to know even Jesus prayed like that gave us confidence to do the same. "Not our will, but Yours be done, Lord."

Rosi

Our friend also referred to the parallel account of this moment in Luke's gospel. The difference between these accounts is the arrival of some angels coming to strengthen Jesus at His moment of supreme stress. It struck me in a new way that if Jesus needed His Father to send angels, then we do even more. Moments of supreme stress are a trigger for God's messengers to accompany His children and bring them strength. If He could do it for Jesus, perhaps God would do the same for us. The stressful moment I had in mind was the committal of Esther's body in the crematorium. Did we have the right to ask for angels to help us there? I even wondered – did angels attend Esther as she left this world? Were they there at her bedside as she slipped into unconsciousness? The thought of her suffering alone filled me with recurring dread and I needed to discover a way to process all this. As a Christian I am comfortable with the reality of angels but I felt a real need to actually believe that they were real and would be there for us. I wasn't quite sure as yet, but I hoped it would come.

As we encountered old friends we recalled the trivia as well as the traumas of our lives in Chichester. Cycle trips, places we'd visited, games we'd played, all had the effect of putting life into perspective. Worshipping in the building where so much of Ian's ministry had been fruitful helped us to see that sadness need not be the dominant colour of our future.

4

On View

*I can look back at different times in my life when I
felt I could not find my way out of whatever it was.
I wanted to disappear. A lot of that has to do with
being in the public eye. (Amy Grant)*

Rosi

It felt as if the world was watching us. Cards and messages were pouring in from people we hardly knew and we felt as if we were surfing a wave of sympathy. We were still only beginning to come to terms with the reality that Esther's earthly life was over. There would be no more new experiences, no more additions to our bank of memories and no more nightly phone calls to anticipate.

Ian has conducted countless funerals in his career as a minister and in almost all of them there is a tribute to the person who has died. Some tributes are the briefest of summaries of a person's life while others are long, detailed and occasionally funny. Most are unexpectedly revealing. These tributes often reveal more about a person at their funeral than we ever discovered while they were alive. Now we faced the daunting task of compressing our memories of Esther into a tribute for her two thanksgiving services.

The Road Not Chosen

No parent ever anticipates doing this. We looked at each other over the remnants of a meal. "Where on earth do we start?" I said. There was silence between us as we puzzled over how to begin. Neither of us could bring ourselves to make the first suggestion. As we goaded our tired minds into action, we began to tap into the wealth of memories but came down to earth with a jolt. It was agonisingly difficult to decide what to include and what to omit. Sometimes tension between us bubbled to the surface, especially over what we should leave out. The talk soon landed on Esther's diabetes.

"I really can't write this," I sighed. "It's like telling the world about something she wanted to keep so private."

"We have to say *something*, after all it's the very reason she died. There's no way we can leave it out."

"But that's almost like betraying her trust! She knew very well we wouldn't intrude into her private space and now we're broadcasting it to the world!"

"The world," Ian curled his fingers into quotation marks, "needs to know why she died. People don't just fall off the planet these days, do they? And anyway, we've been telling people she had diabetes without a second thought, haven't we?"

"Maybe we shouldn't have."

"Hmph." Ian shrugged. Clearly we were not going to resolve this right then.

"By the way, who's going to read all this? Are you, am I, is Ken? I'm really not sure I can cope with it in front of everyone. You know I'm not keen on being on the platform."

It took some more debate but we decided we would swap voices to ease the burden on one another, rather like the way we've written this book. Chris had asked if he could say something about his sister too, so we settled on all three of us reading in sequence. Initially we thought that we wouldn't be composed enough to read anything ourselves, but as we considered what might show the greatest respect to Esther, we felt we needed to face this as a family.

Ian

If Rosi found it tough to write about Esther's diabetes, I found it just as hard to compose a paragraph about her music. Her piano playing was something I missed intensely. Our family piano, which had been her refuge in times of stress, now lay silent, and her crystal clear singing voice would never be heard again in our living-room.

Along with the tribute, I was working on selecting pictures. These would be displayed on a screen above us as we spoke in church, and again there were yet more choices to be made. I wanted to have an opening image that would grab the attention and, if possible, lighten the moment. As I sifted through hundreds of images in my mind, there was only one image that fitted the bill – a childhood picture of Esther, tousle-haired and with a beaming smile. It was unkempt and innocent but above all it said one thing – joy. Here was a blissfully happy girl who was completely unaware that her hair was all over the place and the remnants of a good picnic lunch were spattered around her mouth.

This selection process was going well until I wanted to include pictures from her time in Bolivia. Search as I might they were nowhere to be found. Now in normal life this would be little more than an irritation. But with my emotions constantly running at fever pitch, it now became a major frustration. "Blow you, Esther! Why couldn't you have left things tidy! Everything is in such a mess!" Even when I'd located them on an unmarked CD, I still found shuffling through her images distressing.

The Road Not Chosen

As a church leader I'm aware bereaved families find writing a tribute to their loved one to be one of the more difficult parts of a funeral. Now I was experiencing it first-hand. Questions about what to put in and what to leave out take on enormous importance. We wanted to give an honouring and positive account of our daughter's brief life.

Timing became another source of tension. "How long does this need to be?" Rosi asked.

"I usually give people about five minutes, seven tops, although they often take ten anyway."

"But look at all this!"

She pointed to our pages of notes. "How can we possibly condense this into seven minutes?"

I had to agree with her. It was not just difficult, it felt cruel. How can Esther's preciousness to us, our love for each other, the experiences of joy and pain, possibly be conveyed in so few words and pictures? Her influence still lives through the people she touched and what she believed. That's the true nature of her legacy, but we felt it was demeaning to compress it so tightly. And now we were forced to make choices about what was most important in her brief span of life. I so wished it could have been longer. Or was I being so arrogant in thinking we have a God-given right to live into old age? I was rediscovering how important is every single day, and living as if I could be taken on any one of them.

"What about putting the big things in the tribute first?" suggested Rosi. "Come on, I've heard you use that jar illustration so often. Put the big stones in the jar first and then the little ones and the sand will all fit round it. Am I right? Or am I right?"

She was right. She leaned across the table and we kissed.

On View

Returning to Glasgow

Rosi

It was the evening before the Glasgow thanksgiving service and we were again on the budget flight from Gatwick. It felt strange to be going to the city with a purpose for possibly the last time. What further need would we ever have for this journey which in times past had always held out the prospect of joy and fun with Esther?

Our reason for flying a day in advance of the Glasgow thanksgiving service was pacing. We knew the day would be a heavy one, and to squeeze an early morning flight into our schedule would have added too much to our emotional programme.

We ambled through the centre of town, on to the river bank and along the towpath, all paths where Esther walked for miles. We trudged through the bustling and the tranquil as she had done, sometimes talking but often in silence. On foot in Glasgow, it seemed that every street belonged to her, every view had been seen with her eyes, every road pounded by her feet. Somehow Esther was imprinted on every building. We were tourists in her world, not our own, and we were in this world to say goodbye.

Ian

We were trying to get some answers about how she died and why. Some of those answers might be in the church, others in the university or the place she worked, so we had crammed visits to all three into our schedule. The last item on the agenda was the thanksgiving service itself. Gasping for a coffee, Rosi pointed me in the direction of a café at the back of a bookstore. I entered without taking much notice of the surroundings.

"Just look around, Ian, this was Esther's favourite bookshop." And suddenly the place took on a heightened aura. There was a smell of printed paper laced with the aroma of freshly ground coffee. It had the comforting sense of being one of her spaces, but that only emphasised the painful reality of her absence. It seemed to me that so much of what we were experiencing spoke of finality and completion; retrospect in place of prospect. It's strange how the comforting and the painful can nudge up to each other.

The day Esther had slipped into unconsciousness, she was supposed to have worked a shift at a local nursing home. We planned to visit the home as there were wages outstanding and they were keen we collected them in person. For our part, we wanted to meet the people who worked alongside her and to get some sense of the person she was to them. Esther loved her job.

"Dad, I must tell you about Bert, he's such a sweetie!" she'd said in one of her nightly phone calls. "He can't do much for himself but he's always so happy with life and asks about me and my course and stuff. He's got a wife called Doris who's in the home too and yesterday, while Jean and I were looking after him, he looked me in the eye and got all serious. Then he said, 'Esther – you will look after Doris for me, won't you?' Of course we're doing that anyway, but he's dotty about her. It was sooo sweet!"

A few days later we'd had another call from Esther. This time she sounded crestfallen. "It's really sad, Dad, I went into work today and Bert wasn't there. He died a couple of days ago. I know he was a client, but I really miss him. And Dad, it's all over the newspaper. It turns out he used to be the manager of Scotland's football team – and I was his carer!"

Esther would tell us about other clients she was looking after with enthusiasm and compassion. At the time she had landed this job, she had been looking at other care homes. She had opted for Canniesburn because, "I like the atmosphere in the place and the attitude of the staff to the residents. They really care about them." So as we entered the home we wanted them to know how much Esther had enjoyed the experience of working on their team.

"I really want to try and understand this place," Rosi commented as we signed in. The characteristic fragrance that wafts through the air of almost every nursing home was filling our nostrils. "She seemed to blossom in this job. Something in Esther came alive in this building and I'd love to find out what it was."

Esther could be highly sensitive to the atmosphere of a room or an organisation and would act accordingly, although reading individual people's feelings could be very difficult for her. But here, among people who could do so little for themselves, she had found a niche.

Rosi

We were beginning to notice how our experience of loss was drawing out the pain in other people's lives. Even the manager began telling us about her own struggles, and we found ourselves comforting her and seeking to give her hope for the future.

Esther's line manager had only just heard she had died and was in the early stages of coming to terms with it all. She had found herself on the end of Esther's sharp wit and there seemed to be a genuine respect, even affection, for the person Esther was.

"She was a really hard-working carer, and always happy," we heard. "And she was dead cheeky." Now that was a comment we didn't expect to hear. "Last month I got some figures wrong and Esther picked it up when she checked. She just changed them without any fuss – and then said I ought to go back to school! But there was this grin and such a glint in her eye and you couldn't help love her for it!" She paused. "I'm really going to miss her, you know."

We were beginning to see at first hand some of the complexity of Esther's character. Some of her difficulties with relating to people and her intense desire to withdraw from personal contact seemed to disappear the moment she went through the door of the nursing home. We will share some of this with you later in our story, but for now you just need to know we were meeting as many questions as we were settling.

As we walked away from the home, we pondered together: "If Esther had stayed at this job, she could have been blissfully happy. It may have been an entry level care job, but it brought her fulfilment and joy." It gave her a sense of purpose in life which transcended her problems for so brief a time.

Ian

I was finding the commonplace taking on heightened significance. For us, dinner in a Morrisons supermarket would not normally be significant, but as I sat in the restaurant sharing a panini with Rosi, I couldn't get the uncanny thought out of my head that we were sitting in the place where Esther did her shopping. This wasn't a Glasgow Morrisons, it was Esther's Morrisons. Our daughter had trudged these aisles, queued at these checkouts and probably eaten these paninis. In a strange way grief makes you regard the ordinary as special and adds connections between things and people that no-one else is aware of.

On View

Saying thank you in Glasgow

Ian and Rosi

St George's Tron had become Esther's spiritual home. She had grown to love the place and its people. The church had offered us a room in which to hold a thanksgiving service so Esther's friends and colleagues could say goodbye.

"How many people do you think are likely to come?" the secretary had asked us.

"That's really hard to say. If all the students on her course turn up, which we doubt, there will be about twenty, a few from the staff and any friends of hers from church. I guess about fifty should do it."

"We've got just the room for you!"

While Ian was setting up, Rosi chatted with the students who, in jeans and hoodies, were turning up for the service. They clearly felt awkward about being in the presence of Esther's parents and didn't quite know what to say. We found ourselves taking the initiative again, asking them about themselves and how they were connected to Esther. Strong emotions lay just beneath the surface and consoling these people who had come to remember our daughter became our focus. Here we could honour Esther by comforting her friends.

"I don't get it," said one of the students, his eyes scanning the room as if in an alien environment. "It could have been me. I just don't know what to say." And he shuffled away to find his seat.

It struck us that these young students, who had all of life ahead of them, had had their foundations shaken by the loss of one of their own. The service they were about to experience would compassionately lift them out of any sense of complacency and reveal the uncomfortable reality that life hangs by a thread. Many of the students had come in response to posters that had been dotted all over the university department announcing the service. On each poster was a picture of Esther and the basic details of place and time, followed by a suggestion of an "Esther White dress code of sweatshirt and jeans." The dress code knocked any residual formality out of the window.

The room we had been given could seat about ninety people and they had laid out seventy chairs. Large canvas landscapes hung on the wall, and music from one of Esther's favourite bands played softly in the background. Our estimate of fifty people turned out to be completely inadequate. By the time the service began, the room was full to bursting. More chairs were shoehorned in and people shuffled to find a place to stand. They stood around the walls, crowded in the doorway and used every available space the room had to offer. Scanning the crowd, we could see that most were in their twenties. Some were comfortable being in church, while for others this was an alien environment. Recognising so few people in the congregation we felt like the celebrity visitors, which in one respect we were, but it was celebrity by proxy. We were there on Esther's behalf.

Ian

Esther's tutor stepped nervously to the lectern and took in the room. As she began speaking we were struck by the warm-hearted tone of her tribute. Painstakingly she summarised Esther's academic progress but it soon became clear these facts were only there to give context. When the tutor began talking about the students' visit to Cambodia, her words took a different turn. Esther's character and faith were now at their heart. At several points she became tearful (and I wanted to come to her rescue but that would have been inappropriate). There was courage in her message as she showed she shared Esther's faith in Christ.

"I was looking for some words to say about Esther's life," she concluded. "Some final verses from Esther's favourite book, the Bible, seem so obvious. They talk of a deep thirst, one of the first symptoms of diabetes, and how it may be quenched:

> Come, whoever is thirsty, let him come, and whoever wishes, let him take the free gift of the water of life. (Revelation 22:17)

Esther had a strong Christian faith and knew she was running the race of life with a single aim – to complete it. I believe she would be delighted for everyone here to know she has now completed it ... successfully."

Once again my thought life went into overdrive. Why does our race continue while hers is over? Why did God move the finishing line back down the course for Esther? How can we reconcile our convictions about a loving heavenly Father with the cruel removal of our daughter? I thought I should know the answers to these questions but I didn't. At least, I had no answers that would satisfy me in any more than an academic sense. There is the world of difference between a philosophical understanding of pain and the process of living through it. I needed to voice these questions somewhere, even though I knew there were no simple answers.

Rosi

Our tribute lightened the mood a little. Funny pictures of Esther as a child and teenager could do nothing else and we both felt that its message carried weight. I was particularly concerned that I'd be able to get from start to finish without breaking down. I did, and we noticed how the audience was listening intently, locked into every word.

Ian

The same atmosphere was present when Willie Phillips began preaching. His message was a masterclass in relevant application of the Scriptures. John's gospel describes the moment in Jesus' life when He has just revealed His impending death to His worried disciples. Using John chapter 14 as his springboard, Willie talked about Jesus being a friend.

"Jesus knew His friends were deeply worried, as many of us are," he reasoned. "But a true friend wants to enjoy your presence whether it's in the virtual world like Facebook, or the real world like Costas."

As Jesus' friend, Esther had been called into His presence. Willie couldn't have been clearer about the reality of the gospel and Esther's example of living it out, in spite of her difficulties. He gave the glory to the Lord, not to himself, or the church, or even Esther, but to the Lord Esther served so faithfully and loved so dearly. I'm convinced she would have wanted that to be the emphasis.

We wanted to spend time with people after the service but I was not quite sure what was expected of me. Here was I, a grieving father, shaking hands with people as if I'd just led a Sunday service. Knowing an airport taxi was waiting to whisk us away got me trying to speed up the process. I even caught myself thinking, "How can I shake this person's hand quickly enough to get on to the next one?" I couldn't decide whose agenda was being served here: mine, theirs, Esther's? The taxi came as a place of solace, another little oasis in the turmoil.

"D'you realise this might be goodbye to Glasgow for good?" Rosi said. "Will we ever want to return when so much of the city is associated with Esther? I'm really not sure."

Only time would tell.

Cremation

Ian

When someone comes into your life for a few years, wins your heart and then leaves, how can you honour that? I have already shared with you some of my misgivings about cremation and how Rosi and I agreed to opt for cremating Esther's remains. Some Christians still hold reservations about being cremated, feeling that it prevents the fulfilment of the Scriptures which give us an assurance of resurrection at the second coming of Christ (1 Corinthians 15:42–49 is one such passage). But it seemed to us that the Bible's dominant promise is ultimately of a new body, not a recycled version of the old one. So does it matter what happens to our remains in the process? Burial is a very slow process of decomposition and cremation is a rapid one, but the end results are similar. What is more, many martyrs have been burned for their faith and we honour their memory for it. I felt sure God could resolve the chemistry. This, along with the idea that Esther's ashes could then be scattered out in the country where she loved to run, persuaded me it was the right thing to do for her.

It was a long wait until the hearse arrived with Esther's body. It drew up in virtual silence, gliding to a stately halt in front of our house. Chris and Polly, Rosi and I were waiting inside, dressed and ready to go. But when the doorbell penetrated the silence, none of us wanted to move. I felt it was my role to go to the door and allow the proceedings to begin.

The Road Not Chosen

There in the slightly unkempt driveway, standing beside a leafless tree, was Jenny, the undertaker. As if seeing an old friend, I felt reassured by her presence. She and I had worked on funerals in the past and I knew her to be experienced, compassionate and unflappable. And she was a woman. There was something in me that wanted to respect Esther's femininity, and I didn't want her remains to be swept along in the process-driven male world of undertaking. I couldn't think of a more appropriate funeral director.

Inside we prayed together and again I couldn't control my crying. Jenny had arrived a few minutes early and was very patient with our last minute faffs.

As we walked through the hallway to the waiting limousine, I heard Rosi's gentle voice from behind me.

"Ian, do I look all right?"

"Darling, you look beautiful."

Rosi

Stepping outside the door and seeing the hearse filled with the wickerwork coffin had an air of unreality about it. Could that really be Esther in there? I knew it was only her body and not her person and was surprised at how large the coffin was. Its neatly woven rounded ends made it look less stark, less angular and more ladylike than a traditional coffin. Esther was not a girl or a body; she was a woman, and in this choice we were respecting her femininity.

Arriving at the crematorium, we were met with an enormously long line of black-clad mourners. No hoodies and jeans here, then. As we emerged from the limousine nobody spoke to us. It was as if no-one had anything to say. We found ourselves wanting to smile at them to assure them that, although we were grieving, we were facing this as best we could and this was a time when their support meant so much to us. I felt a deep need to go to my Mum and give her a hug. To reassure, to receive comfort? Who knows? Who cares?

Our immediate family opted to follow the coffin into the chapel so we were ushered into a waiting-room while everyone else filed past the door to find their seats, largely in silence.

Ian and Rosi

We chose to play no part in the committal, so we'd asked a long-standing friend and experienced minister to handle this service. We trusted Eddie implicitly with this moment.

"The reason we're here," he assured the congregation, "is to bring glory to our Maker. For anyone who believes in Christ, even in the simplest way, heaven is our destiny. And that's why we have so much to thank God for when we think of Esther." With exceptional tact and clarity he harmonised the mercy of God and the mystery of death, particularly the death of someone so young.

Now, at the time of writing, we look back in retrospect at the committal and much of it is a blur. People sang heartily, words were said with grace and dignity, but the detail is largely forgotten. Losing these memories may be God's way of applying an inner anaesthetic to our wounds. But we can still recreate the atmosphere in our mind's eye. With Eddie standing in the eggcup-shaped pulpit, we felt secure. Here was an accomplished minister and seasoned pastor bringing the reality of hope and the prospect of healing in Christ.

Ian

The design of the chapel requires mourners to file close to the coffin on the way out of the room. We had elected not to have curtains closing around the coffin as the words of committal were read. This is something many people find to be traumatic in its finality, and we felt there might be people who would feel that in our service, including us. So now we found ourselves first in line on the way out. It's hard to describe the extremity of sadness I experienced as we walked past the intricate basketry of her coffin. This really would be the last I would ever see of Esther, and I felt an intense urge to reach out and touch her for one final time. For some reason I suppressed that urge but found those two words echoing through my heart again. Under my breath I whispered them once more.

"Goodbye darling."

And it was out into the chilly sunlight of a February day.

Why is life so cruel? God, what on earth are You playing at? I had been in this crematorium so often that the room was like a second office to me. But this was no ordinary workday and my attempts to stifle tears were to no avail.

"Where do we go now?" asked Rosi, and I pointed the way to the greeting area.

Rosi

We have never hugged so many people in our lives. It was intensely loving and supportive. For the girls Esther had grown up with, it was their friend in that basket; for others it was their cousin, their niece, and for Chris, his sister. We were not the only mourners by a long way. We had so many people who wanted to hug us, assure us and show their love, that the undertaker had to ask me to get a move on. We could tell that the next funeral had already begun and the last thing I wanted was to start hugging the wrong mourners by mistake!

While on the journey to the hotel, conversation was normal, laughing about Chris's antics while learning to drive. Jenny and the driver were also smiling and lightened the mood considerably. We had chosen a seafront hotel to entertain our family for lunch before the main service began. I'm sure the business guru who chose the title "The Big Sleep Hotel" did not anticipate the irony of having a funeral meal on the premises. On one level it felt like any other family get-together but the reason for us being there was always in the background like ambient music, oscillating between a whisper and a shout. Lunch came and went but again we found ourselves comforting the comforters.

Saying thank you in Eastbourne

Ian and Rosi

It was disconcerting to go into the church where Ian serves as senior minister for a service where our own family was the focus. By nature we seek to keep our family in the background so all this attention felt unnerving. On the way into the service we paused for a prayer together, to invite God's presence as we faced one of our toughest moments. We walked to the front of the church in a hushed silence and took our seats where mourners usually sit. Other members of our family were a couple of rows away and, although we're sure it was not intended, this emphasised the isolation we felt. As the service got underway we were both conscious of God's presence in the building, and Ian's colleague handled leading the service with sensitivity and joy, even quipping about Ian taking charge of a transition into the Bible reading. Clearly old habits die hard!

Ian

We particularly wanted Esther's cousin Lizzie to sing during the service but were unsure which piece of music to suggest. Having gone down a list of options, I had run out of ideas.

There was little time to prepare anything new so I asked her, "Is there anything you've got up your sleeve that would fit?" After a moment's pause, she said, "Actually there is. I've just been rehearsing a song about heaven."

A shiver went up my spine as I became aware of another coincidence with God's fingerprints all over it. The song itself could not have been more appropriate. Its wording spanned so many facets of Esther's life and even included a line about her being given "for such a time as this" – a phrase used of Queen Esther in the Bible.

The church was packed and as we mounted the platform to do the tribute, an expectant hush fell over the congregation. What we feared could be an emotionally wrenching experience turned out to be a time full of God's peace and security. We felt God was answering our prayers again.

A few weeks previously Esther had fallen in love with an old hymn "Count your Blessings". In the weeks in the run-up to her death, this song had become her mantra. Actually it became one of her obsessions as she would play it over and over again to whoever was willing to listen. There was no other way we could end our tribute to her than to get the congregation to sing what had become Esther's anthem.

> Count your blessings, name them one by one
> and it will surprise you what the Lord has done.

Rosi

We had always wanted the service to be honouring to Esther, glorifying to God and a witness to our friends, so we were humbled and delighted by the way this prayer was answered. The reactions to the service were very moving. "This was the best service I've ever been to," said one of our friends. My manager was clearly deeply moved by it all and was close to tears when I spoke to her on the door. Another colleague was similarly affected by it, even though she didn't share our Christian faith. A lady who had just become a Christian at our church said, "I never realised that there are so many positive things we Christians can say about death."

We were amazed at how many people from our past had taken the time out on a working day to come. It seemed that they wanted to identify with us, as many of them had children of the same age as Esther. We lost count of the people we spoke to, hugged, kissed and shook hands with. At times it was almost overwhelming.

Ian

For so many people a funeral is a gloomy occasion to be avoided whenever possible. The intense focus on death's finality doesn't sit comfortably with our society's need to avoid pain at all costs. In a poem called "The Wish", published in 1867, Matthew Arnold wrote:

> Spare me the whispering crowded room,
> The friends who come and gape and go,
> The ceremonious air of gloom –
> All, which makes death a hideous show.

I wish I could have taken him to Esther's thanksgiving service. We avoided calling it a funeral for the very reason that we had so much to thank God for, and we left with a dawning sense that her short life had not been purposeless. We had been in an atmosphere a universe away from Arnold's cynicism and we left as grieving parents uplifted by the combination of joy and solemnity the service captured. It took us a long time to get away from the church, and two friends afterwards told us that the way we were coping was a witness to many people. While this was comforting, we also felt it was a responsibility and a peculiarity of being Christian leaders. This responsibility was to weigh more heavily on us in the future.

Rosi

We had been concerned that just returning to our empty house by ourselves could be heavy and dominated by talk about the day with all its sadness. So it was time for a diversion. I come from a family of six and we were all famished, so an invitation to our house for some food was greeted with enthusiasm. Soon our home was bustling with family and a typical clan meeting ensued. I was in the chair but it was soon out of control with everyone chipping in their ideas about what to eat for tea. The problem was a simple one – nobody wanted to appear selfish. Everyone wanted to be sensitive to everyone else's wishes and the result was complete confusion! Someone had to pin down the chaos somewhere, so Chris and Ian entered the fray and began to intone the entire menu from the local Chinese takeaway, item by item. When they reached item 33 on the menu, no-one was any the wiser. So since nobody seemed to be objecting to Chinese, we placed an order for anything for this number of people and half an hour later we were tucking into a banquet. Only the brave used the chopsticks.

The sense of relief that the day was behind us created uninhibited hilarity. We hadn't laughed as much since Esther had died. I wondered internally whether all this banter was appropriate but quickly rejected that thought in favour of the idea that Esther would have enjoyed sitting in that room being the people watcher and occasionally adding her sharp wit and wisdom to the meal.

5

Good Grief?

The first thing that we need to say is that God is grieving, too. Uh, a lot of people try to make it sound like "well everything that happens is God's will." That's nonsense. (Rick Warren)

Jesus wept. (John 11:35)

Ian

"Darling I've never seen you cry like this before." With those simple words Rosi summed up what was going on in my heart. Wave after wave of weeping would roll over me at the most unexpected and embarrassing moments. I suppose, like many men, I liked to think of myself as a bit of a superhero, capable of fielding anything life threw at me. But any pretence that I could handle this using my own inner strength had long since evaporated. I had been so preoccupied with planning and organising that the intensity of my own sadness had been subsumed into the effort of making things happen.

So what now? For me, the busyness of organising thanksgiving events was giving way to an aching void. I had become so occupied (perhaps over-occupied) with organisation that the prospect of facing life without Esther had been put on the back-burner. There were still residual business matters to sort out, like her estate, but these could take their time. There were now many fewer tight deadlines to meet, so the matter of what life would look like in the future could no longer be avoided. I knew at some time I'd have to face it, and now it was staring at me every time I looked in a mirror.

The relationship between parents and a child is unique. In one sense our children are an extension of who we are genetically, psychologically and relationally. So when a child of any age dies, part of their parents' identity dies with them. This gives the grieving process some unusual features which we experienced ourselves. It is no exaggeration to say that when Esther died, part of us died too.

Rosi

Spotting God in the little things of life became very important to us at this time. The herbs had grown well in the garden, the car cost less to service that year, and the flowers in the garden were coming on nicely. We would comment on things like this and thank God for them. I would point out coincidences to Ian to help him focus on life more positively and, bit by bit, we sought to build a more mindful way of looking at life.

It would have been easy to let our emotions just go wherever they wanted to, and we had done plenty of that, but we also felt we could help each other by bringing some focus to them. Unhelpful grief can start with emotions that are left unchecked or unaccounted for, and we wanted to steer away from this scenario if we could. Of course each of us is different in the way we handle sadness, so the moments when it's helpful to consciously manage our emotions vary enormously. We felt like emotional surfers, sometimes riding the wave wherever it took us and sometimes swimming in another direction. Consciously trying to notice the good things God was doing was one way of swimming in His direction. The choice of whether to surf or swim at any given moment is highly individual but we found trying to spot where God was at work increasingly reassuring. It helped us reduce time spent wallowing in our pain but it was not always easy, and we didn't always succeed. We found we needed to put conscious effort into our grieving in the hope it would build resilience for later on.

Esther had been living away from home since she was eighteen and had already been making her own life decisions. She had a fiercely independent streak which meant she was going to do things at her own time and in her own way. As her parents, we had wanted to support her in creating a life and a career of her own but, as you will see later on, it did not prove easy for her. She frequently needed support and we were often concerned about her vulnerability. We were now beginning to realise that her no longer needing our care was going to take some getting used to. I particularly found one aspect difficult. For twenty-two years I had loved, encouraged and cared for Esther and the emotion that replayed itself over and over again was, "How can I stop loving her? Where is this love I feel for her going to be channelled now?" It was as if I had a reservoir of caring love that now had nowhere to go.

We have both encountered parents whose grief has become a limiting factor in their lives. Some had created a shrine to their child which remained almost untouched for many years. Others might visit the grave daily, many years after their loss, and would delay or avoid other pleasurable activities like holidays in order to maintain the ritual. I was a little afraid this could happen to us. Grief like ours that is maintained over a long period of time can become debilitating, constantly niggling away at our sense of who we are. We could see how easily we could slip into pathological grieving, so we needed to find ways of coming to terms with our own loss to avoid it becoming all-consuming.

In part it had to do with understanding our identity. Did we want our identity to revolve around being bereaved parents, or did we want to be known in some more holistic light? Yes, we are bereaved parents and always will be; and no, we do not want to "get over it" because Esther's life would then have meant little. But we do want to be people who can use this time in our lives as an opportunity for growth and renewal, however painful that might be. The phrase we had used with the local reporter, "We want this experience to help us be better people, not bitter people", was one we found ourselves saying to each other, even over breakfast.

The Esther White Fund

Ian

It is natural for parents in our situation to want their child's life to live on in some way. But in what way could this be? In God's goodness to us, several opportunities presented themselves.

"Shall we send you some flowers?"

It was a question we'd faced repeatedly while preparing for the thanksgiving services and committal. We felt sure it always came from people who were genuinely concerned for us and wanted a way of expressing their love. But it presented us with a dilemma. In Esther's wardrobe there were no flowery clothes, no lacy underwear, and the only things coloured pink were felt-tip pens. Her default dress code of jeans and a jumper was plain to a fault, and behind her simple dress was a frugal attitude to money. She was so thrifty she would regard any expensive flower arrangements as an unnecessary extra.

You will see later that she loved travelling, especially on trips where she could integrate with indigenous or poor people to bring encouragement and hope by working alongside them. These trips had become defining moments in her life and they gave us the idea for the Esther White Fund. By collecting money that would otherwise have been spent on flowers we could, perhaps, get a couple of other young people out on to mission trips that could change their lives too.

"It's jolly noisy on your end of the phone," I had said to her in one of our nightly calls.

"Yes, Dad, I'm in Morrisons bagging up."

"Shopping?"

"No, just packing. I'm putting people's shopping into bags and they donate some money to us."

"Donate to you? How come?"

"I'm going to Cambodia, Dad." I'm not sure if she noticed the pause or my sharp intake of breath as I processed this news.

"Cambodia? Why Cambodia?"

"I want to see how they use prosthetics. We all want to go and I'm going to share what I raise with the others to help us with our fundraising."

It became a trip that changed her life (and we will tell you more about it later). At that point she had needed to raise funds for her airfares so, after she died, we decided it would be a fitting tribute to divert money otherwise given in her memory to help other young people have similarly enriching mission experiences. That was the origin of the Esther White Fund and we have been delighted by people's generosity. It has meant numerous young people have been able to do mission trips all over the world. Some of the people who have benefited from the fund knew Esther personally and were inspired by her adventurous faith. Two of her friends wrote to us about their trip and the support they'd had from the fund. "We have been greatly inspired by Esther's life and been more focused towards God's calling for us since she went to be with Him."

Capturing memories

Ian and Rosi

We were quickly aware that there were many other people who wanted to give thanks for Esther, and a Facebook group seemed an appropriate way of doing this. We wanted to develop an attitude of gratitude for her life and felt that this was a good way to collect people's thoughts. In her short life she had met a huge variety of people and many of them were regular Facebook users. It was astonishing to read what people had written about her. As we saw these snippets roll in, we were humbled by the vast number of people whose lives she had touched. For someone who could be so shy, this was very poignant. One friend said:

> I knew Esther at her first secondary school in Chichester and we had the BEST time together! I have so many lovely memories of making up a secret language together, spilling about 4 pints of milk on the floor in food tech, singing "Let it be" in music class and setting a piece of machinery on fire in year 8! But most of all I remember crying when she left to move to Eastbourne because she had been such a support to me when I was bullied at school.

> We lost touch until last year when I remembered her and thought I'd try to find her on Facebook and thank God I did because I at least got to have one more silly, lovely conversation with her.

Good Grief?

Ian

Memories are such fleeting things. If you don't catch them they evaporate.

Rosi

When Esther was twenty-one, I was keen to give her something she would value into her adult life. I never set out to create a work of artistic genius, but I wanted something tangible and handmade that went beyond a collection of photographs that would otherwise remain stashed away on a hard drive. Something within me wanted to capture the essence of who Esther was for her twenty-first. So hunting out childhood and teenage photographs, tracking down letters and trinkets, gave me the materials to compile a unique mother's gift to her daughter, something no-one else could create for her. As I crafted this scrapbook, the cutting and pasting, the matching of sizes, colours and backgrounds and even choosing the best fonts took me into a world of my own. Above all we both wanted it to be precious to her. Now looking back on it, I am so glad I carved out the time to assemble it. When we gave it to her on her birthday, she read every page with rapt attention, and from that moment on we knew it had become one of her most treasured possessions.

Now we had it in our hands once again. A simple scrapbook which held a woman's life, her parents' love and a touching record of our daughter's history that could never be repeated. I gazed at it, taking in its pathos, and in that moment it became a source of inspiration. Could I now capture all that had just happened, the love of our friends and the emotions of the events, in another book just like the first one?

In our living-room I spread out all the material I could lay my hands on: photos, Facebook messages, cards, e-mails, trinkets, you name it. It wasn't long before the room was carpeted in it all. Two tables, two sofas, an old sideboard and the floor were all covered and there was still a full box left over. Ian came into the room, tiptoeing his way through the patchwork, and surveyed the chaos. I stood in the middle, cuddling the new scrapbook as if it was already an old friend.

"So you're going to get all of ... this," he motioned expansively with his arms, "into that." And he pointed at the scrapbook I was cradling.

"Yep."

"Bestaluck."

And he tiptoed back the way he came.

Going through all this material was like riding another emotional switchback. I found myself laughing, crying and being deeply moved by these simple words and pictures.

"I am filled with grief that I didn't know you better, Esther," said one of her friends. "Your calm peaceful spirit and your willingness to do whatever is needed were inspiring. I am so deeply sorry that the world has lost someone like you but I know you are with your Father now."

Could this really be our daughter? Message after message, card after card, showed that her friends and colleagues held her in high esteem for her love, her determination and her habit of putting other people's interests before her own. Perhaps it's because I saw her through a parent's eyes that I hadn't appreciated the depth of character others saw in her and it sometimes left me speechless. Over the next few days, scrapbooking became my therapy. Sorting, re-sorting, reading and re-reading what had been written about Esther was gradually helping me to navigate this part of our journey.

Several days and two scrapbooks later, the task was complete and they were ready to keep as mementos. But when friends came to see us, we found ourselves instinctively getting these books out to lift the lid on how things had been going for us. I guess it felt like it was her speaking as we talked about her.

One thing that took me by surprise was the reaction of our friends to these scrapbooks. I had expected they might be of some interest to them, but time and again I would watch as someone pored over each page, taking in its message and walking through that part of the journey with us. Many thought we would keep the scrapbooks private and were surprised when we were willing for them to be seen. But we felt that if Esther's life had been given to us as a trust, it was right to share it with others. Friends, family and even people who never knew Esther found them especially moving, and often said they felt privileged to be allowed to see them.

Hard work

Ian

By this time we had taken several weeks off. Weeks without the responsibility of leading a church or managing a caseload had released us from the consistent demands of people in our lives. This had given us space to adjust to a new reality and we were only beginning to learn what our new life would look like.

It's strange the things you miss. Every evening the phone used to ring and Esther's voice would intone "Hellooo" over the airwaves. So when the phone rang in the early evening, my mind would do a double take. For a split second I'd find myself thinking, "Ah, that'll be Esther," as I reached for the phone. But it was only a split second, nothing more, and reality would soon kick back in. It was the same online. When the clock-chime sound of a Facebook poke rang out from my laptop, I'd think "Esther" by reflex. But it would for ever be someone else.

It was really important to us to be able to return to work in an emotional condition that would enable us to shoulder our responsibilities healthily, and deciding when we were ready was not straightforward.

We had no idea that grieving could be such hard work. I would process some e-mail, meet a couple of people and field a few interruptions in my office and then walk round the corner for a sandwich. But then I'd be exhausted and flop in a chair and find myself falling asleep like a toddler needing a nap. We felt tired most of the time and some normal tasks took much more effort than usual. There was part of us that felt the need for things to be normal again but at the same time we knew they never would be. We found we had to learn to pace ourselves and only gradually return to our previous tempo of life. Grieving was using enormous amounts of our emotional energy and we were noticing how much it affected our physical stamina too.

Rosi

After a month I went to see my doctor. By this time he knew what had happened and was prepared to give me another month of respite. I didn't feel ill but was still finding myself constantly preoccupied with thoughts of Esther and questions about why she died.

"Oh it's quite normal," he said. "You're a loving Mum and I'd expect you to feel like that, and it may not go away any time soon. Can't be easy for you." There was a reassuring tenderness in his tone and I began to feel relieved that my strange feelings of abstraction were somehow typical.

Good Grief?

"I can sign you off for another month if that will help." This seemed an unexpectedly long time to stay away from working, but I left wondering what "normal" meant. The question of what is normal was one we often talked about. Should we allow ourselves to feel tired, angry, distracted, or ought we by now to be beginning the return to life as we knew it before? We found we had to guard against the sense of ought-ness because it creates expectations we couldn't possibly satisfy. We were finding that in grieving there is no programme to follow that guarantees recovery. We had to ride the waves that came our way and lean on God in the rough times as well as in the everyday trivia. In the event I was signed off for another two weeks and, once they were up, we both felt ready to take up the reins again. We felt this choice would work for us but knew that other people had stayed away from work for varying lengths of time.

In different ways we both have emotionally demanding jobs; I as a social worker and Ian as the senior minister of a thriving church. We found once again that the constant repetition of our story and the repeated question "How are you?" were draining. So once again we decided on a few sentences that would describe how we felt. It may appear rather contrived but it made us more confident about being able to cope with our emotions, and Ian in particular felt less desire to dissolve into tears.

At this point the boundaries between the professional and the personal were an asset for me but something of a liability for Ian. None of my clients knew my daughter had died, and had simply been told that I was on extended leave. In fact I chose not to tell any of them, both because they had enough issues of their own and also the bringing of our personal tragedy into the professional frame might skew our working relationship.

The Road Not Chosen

Ian

For me it was very different. In the ministry the boundaries between the professional and the personal worlds are much more blurred. For a church leader the conduct of one's personal life is considered to be a matter of legitimate interest by the rest of church. After all, how can anyone know whether the theology being preached on a Sunday can be lived out in practice, unless they see it exemplified in the personal life of the leader who provides them with their primary source of Christian teaching? I was acutely aware of being under the spotlight. Usually this question "How are you?" is the opening gambit to some other conversation, but I noticed how often I was being expected to give an answer about my innermost feelings. And any old answer wouldn't do. Several times when I fudged a response, the person would come back at me with "... and how are you *really*?" The pressure to be personally revealing at almost any moment (even off duty in a shopping centre) became something I felt I needed to be prepared for.

I felt I was under enormous pressure to grieve well, to show that grief can be coped with victoriously and in a way that rises above tragic circumstances, which would not be possible without the bedrock of Christian faith. But I needed to discover this at my own pace. The hidden agenda behind some of my conversations with well-meaning people in church was, "Please don't collapse, Ian, because if that happens, where else are we going to turn?" All this added up to a feeling that I was expected both to be "real" in the eyes of the watching church (to say things like "Yes I do cry about it") while at the same time rising above the intensity of my own grief ("That's how Christians ought to behave, isn't it?") I doubt very much that these expectations were ever created consciously in the minds of people in the church whom I love dearly, but I felt implicit pressure to bounce back quickly.

Probably too quickly.

Good Grief?

"I'd like to talk to Ian in his pastoral surgery."

It was Jo, my PA, who took the call and with characteristic tact she probed a little to find out what sort of situation we might be facing. "It's a personal issue," he said, and Jo, who knew not to probe any further, dutifully booked him in my diary. In my arena of work a "personal issue" could mean anything and would typically be something big or confidential or both. Major relationship breakdown, serious job difficulties, conflict with other church members or life-limiting diagnoses all come into this category. When the man arrived, Jo showed him into my office. He began like this:

"Are you over Esther now? ... I expect you are! ..." And without even pausing for breath, he went on to regale me with his "personal issue". He spun his story in great detail. His knee had been painful for at least a week and he wanted the pastor to know; in fact he wanted me and the rest of the church to pray for his leg. In the privacy of my office I obliged and prayed for his leg, assuring him I would ask a small group of other people to do the same.

"And by the way, how are you getting on?" he said as he got up to leave. When I lifted the lid a little about how tough we were finding things, he was astonished. For him, Christians ought to be able to rise above tragedy; and ministers of the church doubly so. Surely I of all people should be able to just "praise the Lord" and not feel heavy or sad or at my wits' end. To discover that his church leader was still hurting after a few months was a shock he wasn't quite sure how to process.

Rosi

It was now April and ordinary working life had resumed, with both of us committing ourselves once again to our vocations. The familiar rhythm of office, visits and evening meetings was starting up in earnest with its comforting sense of the commonplace. But as the extraordinary was being sandwiched into the ordinary, there were still challenging encounters on the horizon.

After a few days away with friends, we returned to hear that annoying little bleep telling us there was voicemail waiting. It was the undertaker. "Esther's remains are with us now and we'd like to discuss with you what you would like to do with them." While the message was clear and tactful, its impact was stark. From being a living person, Esther had become "remains", a cardboard box of ash that we now had to "do something" with. It was as if the process of handling her death took away her identity as a living person in discrete steps. A sick girl, a body, a coffin, and now merely "remains". This staged depersonalisation was another aspect we had to come to terms with.

Knowing we had already decided that we would like her ashes to be scattered in a particular area, we consulted the undertaker about the process. It was not good news. To do what we wanted would require permission from the person responsible for the land and this permission, she said, would not be given to us. Crestfallen, we had to rethink our plans. A few hours later, while agonising over which way to turn, we realised that a friend of ours farmed the land nearby. We would lose nothing by asking. With some trepidation, we asked for his permission to scatter Esther's "remains" on his land. "I'd be delighted," he said. "In fact, it would be an honour."

It was a crisp April afternoon as we set off to perform this final rite. Trudging to the summit of the hill, the deep blue sky gave the comforting feeling that summer was on the way, and it seemed that the biting early wind had eased itself for our climb. I carried the heavy bucket with all the stones, Ian carried the box with Esther's ashes, and Chris and Polly walked in step with us as we rounded the edge of a copse to emerge onto the exposed hilltop.

Ian

The twenty-two large rounded stones from our garden represented one for each year of Esther's life. We arranged them to create a simple cross shape on the grass. The cross had become precious to Esther in the last few months of her life as she wrestled with the way law and grace showed themselves in the events of Christ's passion. With a panoramic view of Eastbourne as the backdrop, this rudimentary cross became a simple but fitting tribute to her that would soon dissolve into the environment itself.

Standing on that windy hilltop, I could barely bring myself to do the deed. Having scattered many other people's ashes as part of my calling, there was something too final, something too severe about doing it for my own daughter. So as her Dad's final act of kindness towards her, I started pouring the slate grey dust over the twenty-two stones, watching as the dry ash slithered into the cracks. But after a short while I could go no further and Mark took over. Mark was a good friend who had come to the hill to assist us at this seminal moment. As a vicar himself, he had been part of these occasions before and seemed to be able to read my thoughts. He took out his Bible to read a poignant passage from the Psalms and I was aware that I was once again on the receiving end of someone else's ministry. His gently undulating words brought gravitas and comfort.

We just stood there. This grief-wrenched family – Chris, Polly, Rosi and I – remained motionless for a moment in which time seemed to stand still. There on the top of the hill where we had placed Esther, we saw the wind begin to blow her ash into the distance. We tried to take in the enormity of it all. We'd seen our daughter with all her majesty and complexity reduced in stages to a pile of dry ash that was now wafting on to the breeze. We had released her. The body that had let her down so badly was now a thing of the past.

She was free.

Identity

Ian and Rosi

One of the more curious aspects of losing someone dear to you is that it gets you asking questions about who you are in yourself. As we said earlier, neither of us wanted our identity to be completely bound up with being bereaved parents, yet this was the main message other people had picked up about us. The word had obviously gone round the chat wires and people we barely knew would be saying how sorry they were to hear about our daughter's death. In these moments we wanted to be realistic and honest about our struggles, while bringing our faith in God to bear on the situation as we were experiencing it. When writing to the church in Philippi, St Paul said:

> The peace of God, which transcends all understanding, will guard your hearts and your minds in Christ Jesus. (Philippians 4:7)

And little by little we were finding this to be real. Paul's words helped us to see that it's our relationship with God which promises to protect our minds from descending in a spiral of bitterness and despair. But we still had to hang on to this reality by faith every single day. So who were we? Bereaved parents whose whole existence was dominated by sadness, or wrestling Christians who were trying to see God in their circumstances? Or were we some combination of the two? We were living with mystery and hope in equal measure so we had no desire to pretend our Christian faith was some kind of sinecure.

We didn't want this to be all that people knew about us. But if our experience was to have meaning beyond our own lives, we would need, at some point, to communicate it to other people. We both felt that in order to honour Esther, we wanted our experience to be a benefit to others. While we would never wish this on anybody, we were becoming aware that even our sadness was a gift from God that could be used to help others who might themselves be facing losses. St Paul addresses this issue too:

> Praise be to the God and Father of our Lord Jesus Christ, the Father of compassion and the God of all comfort! He comforts us in all our troubles, so that we can comfort those in any trouble with the same comfort we ourselves receive from God. For just as we share abundantly in the sufferings of Christ, so also our comfort abounds through Christ. If we are distressed, it is for your comfort and salvation; if we are comforted, it is for your comfort, which produces in you patient endurance of the same sufferings we suffer. (2 Corinthians 1:3-6)

One of God's purposes in the suffering of His children (like us) is that they would experience direct and personal comfort from Him; and then, from that experience, impart the same comfort to others. This helped us to view our pain in a different light. Instead of it being something that was an aberration, a mistake, as if God's sovereignty had momentarily broken down, it became something He could use to inject His love and comfort into other people He loved just as much as us. And we had an emerging sense of privilege that we could be His channels.

The Road Not Chosen

Rosi

It was Easter 2009 and my first experience of Spring Harvest since we had been there as a family eleven years earlier – which, we were later to learn, had been the time when Esther had committed her life to Christ. Spring Harvest is a large festival of Christian teaching and music that never fails to move and impress. It really was a special place, especially since Ian was now on their board of trustees. So it was even more special that the first occasion of sharing our experience to comfort others took place at Spring Harvest. The seminar speaker had been talking about how God can use listening to Him and journaling as a way of meeting with Him over significant life events.

For years I had kept a prayer diary, and one day in June of the previous year I had been praying for Esther as usual. While I was using my normal pattern of prayer, I sensed God was saying that something surprising was going to happen in her life. At the time I dismissed it as not much more than a hunch, but I did write it down. A few days later the same happened, and then again a week afterwards.

"Ian, what d'you think about this?" I asked, as we talked together in bed. "Several times lately I've felt God say He's going to do something surprising in Esther's life. I know it's only subjective but it keeps coming back."

"It's strange you should say that, because although I haven't written it down like you, I've been sensing the same. Something exceptional might be going to happen for Esther, and God is behind it."

While this may appear unreliably subjective we have both learned not to ignore God's hunches, especially when they repeat themselves. One night we even played a guessing game.

"What's this surprise going to be, then?" I asked.

Good Grief?

"How should I know! A boyfriend? A windfall?"

"A career change? A new home?"

"Healing? Let's not lose this thought, darling," Ian reassured me. "Let's keep on handing her over to the Lord's care and see what happens."

Now we were at Spring Harvest in a seminar which would provide an opportunity for people to talk about what God was doing in their lives. The speaker finished his presentation and fielded the inevitable questions. Then he asked us to talk with the people sitting close to us about how God was at work in our lives, and to tell the whole seminar group, if we felt God was prompting us to do it. A microphone stood like a lonely sentinel in the centre of the room and soon there was a small queue of people waiting to speak. Then the thing I most feared happened. I felt God was asking me to share our experience with these three hundred people. So in great trepidation I joined the queue. When my moment came, my palms were sweating and my mouth felt as if I'd eaten blotting paper. But the words flowed and I just told it all. The diabetes, the surprise, her coma, her death, and how we were still wrestling with it all.

The effect was electric. Murmurs of affirmation punctuated my speaking and everyone I could see from the microphone appeared to be locked in to what I was saying. At the end of the seminar, Ian and I lost count of the number of people who came to us to say how they had been affected by our story. Some were bereaved parents themselves, others knew someone walking the same path, and I knew something significant had happened in that moment. The story of the road we hadn't chosen was beginning to touch the lives of others and there was a deepening sense of privilege that I was the one who was God's mouthpiece.

Heaven Day

Ian

Esther's birthday was approaching and we knew it would be a difficult "first". We were beginning to learn, sometimes the hard way, that anticipating difficult moments and planning for them helped us cope with times that would be emotionally wrenching. Was it possible to escape Eastbourne to find somewhere to mark her birthday, or would we have to do it with the church watching?

There are times when opportunities just drop into your lap and this was one of them. In 2006 I had been invited to preach for five weeks at a church on Grand Cayman in the Caribbean. Superficially it seemed like preaching in paradise as I fed a hungry church with God's word in one of the world's most exclusive beauty spots. At the time I didn't realise the subtext of their invitation – they were looking for a new senior minister and had me in their sights. So the invitation to consider moving from Eastbourne to take up the reins in Georgetown took us by surprise and got us thinking seriously about our future. Did God want us to move or to stay? Had we completed our work in Eastbourne? And how were we to evaluate God's will for our lives at this moment?

Don't underestimate how tempting this offer was. In other circumstances (and if I was giving advice to someone else) I would be saying, "Seek God about it and, unless He closes the door, grab it with both hands. Don't let an opportunity like this slip through your fingers!" But we were uneasy and felt no peace about it. And in retrospect we can see the hand of God in this tantalising dilemma. Had we been in Grand Cayman when Esther became ill, a trip home could have taken a week to realise and we would have missed those precious final hours with her. We would always have found it difficult to resolve the subsequent inevitable feeling that we had abandoned her in her time of need.

What neither of us expected when we left Grand Cayman was the extent to which we'd left a part of our hearts in Georgetown. In those five weeks the fellowship took us to their hearts, and so later, when we sent e-mails telling our friends our sad news, we were deeply moved by the intensity of their responses. Message after message was filled with love and concern, even though none of them had ever met Esther. One message came from their worship pastor who said (as so many did), "If there is anything we can do, please let me know."

There was. We made a tentative enquiry about going to see our friends in Grand Cayman again and found some flights that might be within our budget. I had a two-word response from the worship pastor: "Book 'em!"

Their kindness was almost overwhelming and the week we spent there genuinely helped us to process all that was going on in our hearts at the time. Sunday May 31st would have been Esther's birthday and we had already decided how we would mark it. For some time we had felt we wanted to write a special prayer thanking God for trusting her to us and for the twenty-two years of her life. We call it scripted praying and there are some notable examples in the Bible.

At key moments of our lives, Rosi and I have crafted written prayers to pour out our hearts to the Lord. Prayer takes so many different forms in our lives and this is one colour in the spectrum. Instead of reading prayers from a book or praying extemporaneously, there are times when we prefer to think carefully about the words or concepts we want to convey to God, write them down and choose a special time and place to pray them. "Heaven Day" is our prayer in which we thank the Lord for Esther. It took us several weeks to complete and there were many tears along the way, but the sentences we crafted gave us a prayer that expressed our enormous gratitude to God for being the parents of such an unusual and precious daughter.

The day on which we would say this prayer was a no-brainer: 31st May. But it wasn't until we'd booked to go to Cayman that we realised the opportunity that God was giving us on the choice of location.

When I had visited Georgetown the first time in 2006 I had been surprised to discover a Baptist church without a baptistery. Such an omission would be unthinkable in Britain and I'd asked one of the church leaders what they did about baptisms. He'd said, with a twinkle in his eye, "You wait and see."

The following Sunday, Louella was to be baptised. She was a lively teenager who had asked to make her faith public. No sooner was the morning service over than several hundred people cascaded out of the building and began walking down the road. The procession was led by Louella, the worship pastor, and Louella's family, each with rucksacks slung jauntily over their shoulders containing swimming gear. It did not take long to work out where they were going. Within walking distance of the church was Smith Cove, a place of exceptional Caribbean beauty where the glitterati go for their photoshoots. This exquisite inlet, with its turquoise water, soft sand and shady trees, provided the perfect place to publicly baptise believers.

This place was significant to us because, although she was ready to be baptised, Esther never took that step. While she was committed to baptism and encouraged her friends in that direction, she never felt able to do it herself. Was it the sense of spectacle or the attention that would come her way? We never knew for certain. It would have been her Dad's great delight to have baptised her in this cove which I regard as one of the most exquisite baptismal pools in the world.

So we prayed "Heaven Day" for the first time on the day which would have been her 23rd birthday. Although it will never touch your soul in the same way it touched ours, we have included it at the end of this book for you to read.

"Heaven Day" was written to satisfy the need in our hearts to be clear with God about how much Esther had meant to us and the legacy of determined faith she had bequeathed to us. We wanted to honour her in the way we lived our own lives from that moment onwards. Praying "Heaven Day" for real was a painful experience and I'm very glad the beach wasn't busy. But it was releasing. It was almost as if I'd baptised her in that cove and set her free to be the woman of God she could potentially have been.

She never heard the applause

Ian

Quite unexpectedly we received an e-mail from Esther's tutor in Glasgow to say the examination board had met and decided that Esther qualified to receive a posthumous Certificate in Higher Education. Would we like to travel to the university on graduation day in November to receive it at a separate prize-giving after the main ceremony? We were very touched by this gesture. We knew we had to go but it meant returning to Glasgow with all its memories.

I felt we had to plan carefully. Receiving this in front of a group of people would be emotionally draining again, so we took the decision to be kind to ourselves and stay on an extra day. This was to be our sad day. We discovered this practice almost by accident and found it very helpful in the process of recovering from loss. I can usually anticipate which are the days when we must hold things together, and avoid collapsing in emotional heaps. We came to call these our brave days. Resilience, determination and bravery are the emotional headlines on these days, particularly when public engagements are involved. But following a brave day, we learned to put a sad day in our diaries. This would include times where we could reflect, be alone and avoid other pressures. If we wanted to talk, we talked; if we wanted to weep, we wept; and if we wanted to tell God how little we understood what was happening, we told Him. We discovered that the strength needed to see us through a brave day was much easier to find if we knew a sad day was coming tomorrow.

The room where the awards were to be handed out was normally used as the communal meeting area in the Prosthetics Department. When we arrived, the room was already packed with students, staff and as many relatives as could be squeezed into the space. We stood near the back. Anatomical diagrams filled several noticeboards and against the wall stood a display cabinet boasting an eerily realistic artificial foot next to an exquisitely engineered wrist joint. So this was another of Esther's domains. I imagined her here, chilling out with her friends, or sitting alone resolutely following through some piece of work, surrounded by a jumble of papers.

There was excited banter as the ceremony got underway, with students from all over the world receiving their awards, many at considerable personal sacrifice. Glancing at the programme we realised we'd been kept until the end. When the moment came, the MC looked over and beckoned us forward. Weaving our way between the seating, we recognised many of Esther's friends and colleagues we'd come to know around the time she died. As I received the certificate, I asked if I could say something.

"Of course," the MC whispered, and promptly announced authoritatively that "Mr White would like to say something."

Good Grief?

As I turned to speak, a hush descended on the room. I thanked them warmly for their support and framed a few sentences about Esther herself. I was conscious that every eye was locked on to me, listening intently as I spoke about her love, her determination and her walk with God. I finished something like this:

> While we're parents who have lost our daughter – and that hurts terribly – we're also Christians who are confident we'll see her again. That's a hope I know she would want all of you to share, whatever background you come from. Rosi and I feel she's left us all a legacy. Not a legacy of money (goodness knows, no student has money these days!) but one of love, determination and, above all, faith in Christ. That living faith was her motivation to do just about everything else. It saw her through her toughest times as well as her most joyful ones. Nothing would please Esther more than to know you might at least consider following her example.
>
> So thank you.

There was a moment's pause as if nobody quite knew what to do, but it was quickly swamped by enthusiastic and sustained applause.

Sitting at the back was the Disability Officer we had met previously, and we were soon deep in conversation once again.

"At times I found Esther something of an enigma," she said.

"I think we all did!" we agreed. Then she continued "... but I saw in her a student of great depth in spite of her difficulties." At which her tone of voice lowered and she revealed, "I often find myself thinking about Esther, and I find myself asking what she would have done in situations I face myself."

Esther probably never realised her own impact, but we'd like to think she would have appreciated the applause.

Carols

Ian

Most churches hold carol events around Christmas time and we were no exception. Making "Carols by Candlelight" meaningful whilst maintaining the sentiment of an enjoyable carol singing event is an annual challenge for any minister. But there are years when a clear opportunity just falls into your lap and 2004 had been such a year. Esther had joined Youth With A Mission as part of a gap year project and was enjoying her first extended time away from home. By the time Christmas came, the South American trip was about to begin. Esther and her team were staying overnight a few miles away in Brighton and wanted to make the trip to Eastbourne for our carol service.

After entertaining all nineteen for tea, I interviewed Esther in the service along with some of the other young people. Any parent who sees their eighteen-year-old head off to rural South America with other teens and twenties is going to have a few qualms. But neither of us could deny the clarity of Esther's sense of calling and her passion about going. As I interviewed her, I heard our daughter talk freely about God's plan in her life, about how she wanted to serve the church in Bolivia and her excitement about going. To be sure, we were justifiably proud of her and grateful to God that she had the courage to stand in front of the church, and also was brave enough to spend nine weeks on the other side of the world. Although we were now five years on, the excitement of that moment was still fresh in my mind.

Good Grief?

Rosi

Back to the present, and the task of crafting Carols by Candlelight 2009 was looming. Ian likes to include personal stories about what God is doing today, along with the conventional "Hark the herald ..." and "Once in royal ..." Real life stories lift the service above the sentimental and add a contemporary impact to the events of Christmas. Another personal story was required about God's faithfulness during the past year and Ian had already scouted around the church for a suitable person. Uncharacteristically, no-one was both available and willing. I had been wondering whether to offer to share our story but had kept it quiet from Ian.

"Darling, what about me?" I finally asked over breakfast. By default we try to avoid drawing attention to ourselves in church and this would be a highly public moment. Ian thought for a second.

"Do you think you could manage it? It's going to mean talking about Esther, and very publicly, all over again."

"I think it will be good to share our story. It'll also give us a chance to say thank you to the people in the church again. What you do think?"

The service was packed, the church lit by hundreds of candles, and as I mounted the platform, there was a hush. I think people had an inkling of what was coming. These were my friends. These were the people who had loved us through the traumas, and I wanted them to know how much we appreciated them and how they had helped us hang on to God in the toughest of times.

"Five years ago at this very service our daughter Esther stood right here to tell you about the calling of God on her life. She shared with us the reality of God's faithfulness and the ways He provided the things she really needed. Most but not all of you will know that in February this year Esther died and went to be with the Lord she told you about. I hardly need to tell you this has been the most difficult year of our lives and we have not 'got over it' by a very long way. But tonight I want to share with you the same realities that excited Esther: God's faithfulness, God's provision and His love for us – even when life gets unbearably tough."

And once again I just told it like it was and let the events speak for themselves. People listened in rapt attention as I retold the story. When I had read it through at the rehearsal before the service, it almost felt that it was someone else's narrative, but at the actual event it felt as if God was speaking through me. I particularly wanted to tell our story to the people who only go to church once a year, and I would love to know if my experience made a significant impact on any of them.

I may never know for certain, so all I can do is trust.

6

Esther's Journey

Sometimes it's the journey that teaches you a lot about the destination. (Sir Francis Drake)

"I know the plans I have for you," says the Lord, "plans to prosper you and not to harm you, plans to give you hope and a future." (Jeremiah 29:11)

From Day 1

Ian

"**P**lease Lord, don't let our child be born just yet." This prayer flashed across my mind as Rosi lay in the late stages of labour. As the stark black-rimmed hospital clock ticked towards midnight, I realised there might be a coincidence that would add an extra layer of joy to the birth. No sooner had I prayed than my mind was shot with a slug of guilt. How could I show such a lack of compassion? How could any caring husband want to prolong the agony of his wife's labour? So when the nurse poked her head round the door and intoned cheerily "How are we doing then?" I wasn't sure how to answer her.

"You're an expert," I said. "Given where we are now, what's your best guess of how long?"

"Oh," she shrugged, "your wife is ready to give birth, so it could be anything from a few minutes to a few hours." Not much guidance there, then. But when we welcomed Esther into the world about four hours later, there was a memory which came flooding back.

It was Sunday morning in 1964 and I had been gripped by my father's preaching in church. His message had been about being born again and the real story behind this much maligned phrase. Jesus had been talking with a Jewish teacher who, in spite of his wealth of knowledge, had never made his commitment to God personal. Nicodemus was a religious expert of impeccable credentials whose relationship with God had yet to begin, and somehow my young mind latched on to this. Being eleven-and-a-quarter and having a pastor as a Dad I was, *de facto*, an expert on religion! But that morning I came to realise that all my churchgoing and trying to be good (whatever that looked like) would count for nothing with God, any more than it did for Nicodemus.

As the warbling of the Hammond organ faded away, I had a very clear impression that I needed to do something about my life and give Jesus Christ a place in it. Some of the congregation shuffled out to leave only the most committed worshippers for communion. Here in sombre reverence they would pass bread and wine round to celebrate Jesus' last supper. This must be for the highly holy people only, I reasoned, because kids like me were strictly excluded. From the other side of a heavy door I could hear the clink of glass on silver, the familiar prayers being intoned and the drone of hymns. Cat-like I paced up and down the side of the church, peeping through a keyhole to see when the end might be in sight. There was more Hammond as the remaining congregation started filing out past my father, each shaking hands with the formality characteristic of the 1960s.

"Goodbye, Mr White."

"Thank you, Mr White."

"I did enjoy your sermon, Mr White."

"Nice to be here, Mr White."

I gatecrashed Mr White.

"Dad! I want to talk!" I urged; and without so much as waiting for the next handshake, he left the queue and ushered me into a side room. It was a postage stamp of a room with elderly wooden chairs, each with its back to the wall. The musty smell of seasoned varnish filled the air. It seemed my father knew instinctively how his son needed help, and with fatherly tenderness he unravelled the mystery of coming to faith, just for me. There was a warmth in that room even though I could see no heater, and a presence I can still feel to this day. Within a few minutes, we were kneeling together at one of the more rickety brown chairs and I was doing what Dad encouraged me to do. I followed him phrase by phrase as he gave me the words of a childlike prayer.

"Now you say just what Jesus said to Nicodemus but this time put your own name in," he said. I obeyed, falteringly, reading the text from the rustling India paper of my King James Bible.

"For God so loved the world that He gave His only begotten son, so that if Ian believes in Him, he will not perish but have eternal life." I paused. "Is that it?"

"Yes, Ian, that's it. You've given Jesus a place in your heart."

It was as if heaven touched earth in an instant and my young mind was flooded with the elation and relief of knowing that the issue was settled. Tears rolled down my cheeks but I felt no shame for my crying, only joy, release, freedom and forgiveness; and as we left the room to return to the church I knew something momentous had happened. I may only have been eleven-and-a-quarter (and I have had to reaffirm that commitment many times since) but that transformational moment changed the course of my life, and I still look back on it as my moment of being born again.

That was 31st May 1964 and this was 31st May 1986, so Esther and I now shared a birthday.

Emerging personality

Rosi

As a little girl, few things pleased Esther more than creating dens and houses out of bedclothes, curtains, clothes dryers and anything else which came to hand. If we went upstairs to find the bed stripped, the towels missing and a trail of pegs littering the landing, we knew Esther was building.

"Where are you, Esther?"

"I'm in my palace," a little voice would say from inside her latest construction.

"So this is a palace, eh?"

"Of course it is, Mummy, can't you tell? This is where the king sleeps ..." She would point to my pillow, wedged neatly into a corner. "And this is where the queen makes her dinner." She motioned to a mock kitchen meticulously designed out of other toys laid out on a flattened tea towel. Even when she was very young there was an intensity to her creativity we all admired. If Esther was in charge of the building, every item, down to the tiniest peg, had some significance. Nothing was left to chance.

About this time I was leading a parent and toddler group in the church where Ian worked. This meant I was often distracted with the organisation and operation of the mornings, and Esther, although no longer a toddler, would have to amuse herself. This gave her the opportunity to develop her flirting skills. Making full use of her large blue eyes, she melted the hearts of the coffee servers to wangle a steady supply of biscuits out of their hands, which she then shared with other children who were also left to play. Generosity was to become one of her hallmarks.

So too was a love of board games. It would take the briefest of suggestions for Esther's face to light up and for her to gleefully rummage in a cupboard crammed with our family games.

"Game?" (I only needed to use the one word.)

"Game," came the response; and soon the table was full of the paraphernalia of Payday, Esther's game of the month.

It was the end of a long day which had left me exhausted but Esther still had energy to burn. She had taken on herself the responsibility of making sure the pieces arrived at the correct places on the board after each play. No sooner had the first few plays been completed when my eyes started to droop, and soon I was dozing between turns. I don't remember the next twenty minutes but I woke to discover Esther continuing to play for her snoozing mother, who was now winning the game. This quality of sacrificial honesty was one that would stay with her into adulthood and would lead her to make sacrifices for other people that would sometimes leave her at a distinct disadvantage.

The Road Not Chosen

Ian

"Oooh, it's a death slide!" Our son Chris was tugging at my coat as we took in the scene at a theme park. It was our first time at this particular venue so every attraction represented a new adventure. Like greased lightning, he ran in the direction of the slide and I saw him disappear through the door at the bottom of the building. He leapt up the stairs with me panting in hot pursuit. By the time I caught him up, he had got to the top and was looking over the edge. Pondering the void, his little face scrunched as he became more convinced throwing oneself off a cliff was not such a good idea. If he was a little nervous, I was terrified, not just for Chris's safety but because I could hear Esther's little footsteps plodding up the stairs to meet us.

At this point I faced a dilemma. Should I do the man thing and show them how it's done? If I did, they would be left unaccompanied on the edge of a sheer drop; so I rejected that idea as irresponsible. Should I advise caution and retreat down the stairway? But that would leave them disappointed and leave me, as likely as not, cast in the role of spoilsport. While I was weighing up both sides in my inner debate, Esther barged in front of me and, to my amazement, took her place on the lip of the slide. My heart leapt into my mouth. Here was my five-year-old daughter standing on the edge of a twelve metre near-vertical drop. All the nightmarish scenarios of uncontrolled falling, broken limbs and intense pain came flooding into my mind. My instinct was to grab her for her own protection but I needed to keep the situation cool in spite of the turmoil raging within. Adopting my calmest tone and speaking my words one at a time so there could be no confusion, I said, "Esther, just come here to me."

Then, as I reached out to draw her back from the brink, she turned, assumed her most authoritative tone, and told me, "This is how you do it, Daddy," and jumped. With a shriek of delight she hurtled to the end of the slide, turned and called out, "Your turn!"

For the rest of the afternoon the death slide was almost the only attraction she played on, obsessively going back and forth, back and forth, back and forth, until the seat of her trousers and the back of her coat were rendered threadbare. This was the first of many examples of genuine bravery we were to see in her. She would show herself unafraid to go out on a limb and try things her peers, and even her parents, might baulk at.

Animals

Ian

We were clambering over rocks by the beach, peering into the curious world of rock pools, when Esther stayed behind, gazing at something.

"Daddy, look at this! It's – a – snail!"

We had already seen a dozen snails on our safari and I was at a loss to know why this one was so special. She crouched over it, transfixed.

"This is Sammy the snail and I want to keep him and look after him," she announced. So, rustling up a jar, Esther created Sammy's world, the most luxurious place a snail could think of. Never has a snail been afforded such affection and love. The jar was constantly replenished with water, seaweed and other goodies Esther chose for him. Sammy's jar would nestle in Esther's lap as she talked earnestly to him as if to a long-lost friend. When Sammy began to accompany us on trips in the car, we started asking questions.

"This snail thing," I would begin. "It's getting a bit OTT, don't you think?"

"Oh she's only six. All six-year-old girls have a pet of some kind. I don't think we need to worry."

"Yeah, maybe, but I think this is all getting a bit intense for someone so young."

"What do you think we should do, then – prise her away from it?"

"Hmm, I can't see that would help really. She's completely besotted. Everywhere she goes, he goes. Even has him in her bedroom at night."

"So I can see that heading home is likely to create an interesting moment for us, then? One thing I'm not doing is taking a live sea snail back to Chichester. How would we look after it?"

When the holiday came to an end, a rather crestfallen Esther agreed to return Sammy to his home. So, taking a detour to the beach where we found him, we opened the jar at the water's edge to let him slither out.

"... and we must pray for him, Daddy."

So a prayer later we watched as the unsuspecting mollusc rolled back into a rock pool just as a wave broke over it. Esther would not be taken from the scene but stood, quiescent, gently waving goodbye as the waves enveloped her beloved friend.

Some years later Esther fell in love with Alex, not a boyfriend but a hyperactive rabbit whom only she seemed able to tame. We had selected it in a pet shop, with Esther giving deep thought to exactly which of the litter on display she should choose. Alex was a pure albino whose white coat and red eyes marked him out as different from his siblings. Esther loved her rabbit with an intensity that spilled over into showering him with gifts.

"I've bought something for Alex," she said one day on returning from school. She was delighted with her new acquisition, and we were keen to see what she was going to produce from her bag. Slowly, as if she was performing the magician's big reveal, she pulled from her rucksack a small ball of tangled plaited red cord and buckles, which she held out for us to examine.

"And this is ...?" I probed.

"It's a harness, Dad," she said, giving me one of her withering looks. She unravelled the ball to reveal a rabbit-sized collar and lead. "Now I can take Alex for walks. After all, we do it for dogs," she reasoned, "so why not my Alex?"

Thereafter Alex was taken for his daily constitutional around the paths of the close where we lived. Esther soon discovered that rabbits and dogs behave very differently on a walk and she became a source of great amusement to the neighbours. She would follow as Alex hopped at random across their open-plan gardens.

Rosi

Alex had been part of our family for over two years when a breakfast-time glance out of the kitchen window revealed that his hutch had been damaged. Esther had not yet emerged from the bathroom, and I went to investigate. Putting my finger to my lips to warn him to keep quiet, I motioned to Ian to come into the garden.

"You need to see this," I whispered. He came, closing the door with a quiet click behind him.

The Road Not Chosen

There, lying on the grass behind his hutch, his legs splayed and his white coat spattered with blood, was Alex. His spinal cord protruded from his neck and a pool of blood was drying on the ground beneath him. He was headless. I glanced around to locate the rest of his body. Under a rose bush on the opposite side of the garden was his severed head, bloodied but intact, with his ears drooped as if in restful sleep.

"For my money, this looks like a fox attack," said Ian. "They're urban savages, if you ask me. Just look at this mess!" His face winced as he surveyed the gore by his feet. "They don't kill to eat, they kill to play. It's barbaric!"

"What are we going to do now? We can't just send Esther off to school. She's bound to come out here to say goodbye to him."

"We'll have to tell her and just do our best to soften the blow. Gosh, this is going to hit her like a brick!"

Esther emerged from the bathroom and our faces told her something was up.

"Esther, come and sit down, darling," we said, trying to make sure she was out of the window's eye-line. "Something has happened to Alex."

"Oh that's no problem! He's got out of his cage before and I've found him alright. We know the garden's rabbit-proof, don't we?" She looked quizzically at me. "Do we?"

"Darling, it's more serious than that. It's not Alex getting out, it's a fox getting in, we think. There's no easy way to tell you this, dear, but Alex has died."

She started to quiver and as I put my arm round her she darted for the door. We followed her to the centre of the lawn where her beloved Alex's headless body lay. For a moment which seemed endless, she stood still, unable to take in the enormity of it. Quietly at first, as if in a world of her own, she began to weep. These were not the tears of a grazed knee or a sprained ankle, but the deep wrenching sobs of a nine-year-old being overwhelmed by grief for the first time in her life. I would have given anything to protect her from the pain of that moment but it would have been fruitless. We had to face this together.

Later in the afternoon, we buried Alex in a garden border plot marked by a simple cross. We prayed, we hugged and we thanked God for the gift of a wonderful friend. Esther may have been a child, but her grief was real and for weeks afterwards she pined for Alex. Something in her died in that moment.

The following morning (and I don't think we ever told Esther this part of the story) we made another gruesome discovery. Pulling back the kitchen curtains revealed that some animal, possibly the same fox, had dug into the grave, pulled out the body and abandoned it in the centre of the lawn. Ian and I scurried around, keeping Esther at the front of the house while we removed the evidence. Then, while Chris and Esther were out at school, Ian buried Alex again, this time much deeper.

From that moment on, the Roald Dahl tale *Fantastic Mr Fox* never had quite the same appeal.

Ian

And if I ever get my hands on that fox ...

I suppose we were naïve to assume that a second rabbit would ever be a substitute for Alex; grieving is rarely assuaged by a replacement. However, when another rabbit came into her life, Esther developed a deep connection with him too, and we noticed how her rabbits were becoming much more than pets to her. We are not a family who put a particularly high value on having animals in the house, so this passion came from deep within her.

"Is he going to have a name?" I asked in all innocence.

"Oh yes, Dad. He's Almeo."

"And where does 'Almeo' come from?"

"Well, it's like this. Al is from Alex, and he's first because I miss him so much; Me is from Mimi my old hamster, and Yo is from Yoyo, the other hamster. So I've got a bit of lots of my pets in his name – especially Alex!"

"Can I stroke him?"

"Of course you can." Her face lit up as we shared this moment of compassion with her new friend. "Actually, Dad, you can do more than that. He's not hyperactive like Alex, he's really ..." she thought for a moment, "... kind of calm. Even old people like you can hold him and he won't run away." And with great tenderness she placed Almeo on my lap.

"Esther." I looked into her eyes as she lifted her gaze from her new pet. "I think he's a lovely rabbit."

"Yes Daddy, so do I."

From then on Esther would sit for long periods of time in the garden with her rabbit cradled on her lap, talking with him at great length. At the time we thought this was just one of Esther's endearing quirks but we were later to realise a deeper significance of these moments of tenderness with her pets.

Music

Ian

As parents, one of the gifts we dearly wanted to impart to our children was a love for music, to whatever sort they felt most attracted.

As a young man I had been severely bullied at school and found music to be my release valve during those disquieting times. Beethoven became my solace and Mozart my mentor as a pain-filled world raged around me. Music had the capacity to take me to a place of beauty and sanity where my emotions could be expressed without fear of reprisal. Should my children face such times of difficulty and sadness, I wanted them to have music as their consolation too.

We tried to fill our home with music and encouraged both Esther and her brother to tinker on the piano, recorder, violin, and anything that could make a tune, even milk bottles! Esther's aptitude emerged in her singing, clarinet and piano playing, and was to be, as time went on, an enormous source of personal joy and emotional release to her. She would spend hours composing and painstakingly writing each note into the family's computer until she had a full score of her piece.

Rosi

But performing was another matter. Only rarely would Esther play any of her material to other people, so intense was her shyness. But curiously she didn't avoid public performance altogether and gleaned tremendous pleasure from singing in a choir. Possibly it was the nature of a choir as an ensemble where she wasn't exposed, or the camaraderie of choral music which inspired her to continue. Singing in *Joseph and his Amazing Technicolour Dreamcoat* with some of the cast from the West End musical sparked her love of music. After the first dress rehearsal she came home buzzing with all she'd seen and heard. From her bag she pulled the top the singers were to wear for the performances.

"Look! I can say I've been there, done it *and* got the T-shirt!" – and from that day on, this T-shirt became one of her most treasured possessions.

But while playing at home, a different attitude was beginning to emerge. She doggedly pursued her piano exams and we could tell she found release and joy in her piano playing. But if she ever detected an audience while she was practising, the concert would come to an abrupt halt. Many times we stood outside the dining-room door admiring her singing and playing, but as the door was opened and we entered, she would find an excuse and the music would cease.

Ian

Now wind the clock forward to a few days before she died. Kit told us that during the week before she went into a coma, Esther could be heard singing at the top of her voice when she was alone in their front room. The hopelessly out-of-tune piano that lived there had become her place of worship. Being a new tenant, he was in awe of the music which filled the air. Esther, oblivious to any audience, sang songs of praise and worship, some of which she had composed herself. It seemed that her closeness to God was often expressed in her singing, and when she was alone in her room she could be so caught up in worship that she didn't care whether there might be other people in the house listening. Through music, she would often lose herself in her relationship with God.

The great outdoors

Rosi

Living in Eastbourne as a teenager encouraged Esther's love of the great outdoors and we often went for long walks and even longer cycle rides to all points of the compass. One of her friends commented:

I'll never forget our cycle rides on Sunday afternoons. We would cycle side by side (and occasionally nearly get run over) and chat and sing. Esther taught me a song she learned on a camp with the tune of *Give me oil in my lamp* but we changed the words to *Give me air in my lungs* etc.

At this time in her life Esther had a carefree side to her nature that showed itself only when she was at her most secure. She was developing as a competent organiser of people. When one of her friends hatched the idea of a camping trip, it was Esther who pulled the equipment and people together. She and her friend Christine planned these trips meticulously, with all the campers having specific, and sometimes quirky, tasks assigned to them. Such essential roles as "flood defence helper", "fly swatter", "gas stove lighter", "chief tent pegger" and "chocolate provider" were all included in their admin. In this group, where she felt secure and at ease, Esther's imagination was often sparked into life. One of the tasks assigned to her was "chief story teller" so that in the evenings she would regale the tent with inventive tales which kept the other campers enthralled.

When, as a university student, she became so withdrawn, it was the knowledge that we had seen her so outgoing and creative that first got us asking serious questions about her mental condition, and what we could usefully do to support her.

7

Developing Faith

Faith is to believe what you do not see; the reward of this faith is to see what you believe. (Saint Augustine)

Now faith is being sure of what we hope for and certain of what we do not see. This is what the ancients were commended for. (Hebrews 11:1-2)

Rosi

In 1998 our family spent a chilly Easter in a basic chalet at Spring Harvest, Minehead. In spite of the spartan conditions we relished every moment, and at one of the youth gatherings Esther made the same commitment to Jesus Christ as Ian had many years before. But so intense was her desire to keep some parts of her life private that she never told anyone. In fact I didn't discover this until several years later, and even then by a circuitous route. She asked me to check through an application form she was completing to take part in a project on which she was asked to write about herself – and there it was.

Following that Spring Harvest event, however, we had easily spotted her developing walk with God. It was not long before her desire to encourage others to follow Jesus for themselves became evident. But she wasn't going to be drawn about any moment of commitment of her own. Here was another part of her life that was locked down from people in her world and was a hint of difficulties to come.

"Mum, some of my friends are coming round on Thursday, is that OK?" The request was not a surprise as she would sometimes invite a friend or two into our home to play or chill out together. This seemed different, however, and sounded as if she was organising. When the evening came, a small clutch of girls arrived and took over the living-room. Gales of laughter wafted through the air, sandwiched by long periods of what sounded like more focused talking.

"Can we do it again next week, Mum?" she asked as her friends left the house in buoyant mood. She looked tired but satisfied and it wasn't long before we realised she had created a group of friends to read their Bibles together, talk about life and pray. After her death, one commented about this group, "She had really helped me to grow in my faith." And another told us, "The strength of her faith has been a great witness to me over many years." Yet another commented, "I looked up to you over the years Esther, you affected more people to the good than you know, I don't think you realised it :)"

She probably didn't.

In search of a mission

Ian

Esther was never afraid to take a bold initiative; in fact quiet bravery was one of her traits that we most admired. She would often spend many hours planning or preparing a project before anyone else discovered what it was. Publicly reticent but privately tenacious was the way Esther approached her world. But now she faced a major question: having left college, what should she do in the next phase of her life? While some of her friends were planning an indulgent gap year to travel the world, she was investigating opportunities that would stretch her faith and serve the underprivileged.

"Dad, if I wanted to do something for a short time that would be with Christians and help other people, what's out there?" she enquired.

"Oh, you could try OM, BMS, YWAM, WEC, AIM or even ECM."[1] She gave me her most withering look.

"Dad, you're talking in code. Decrypt all that for me!" And over the next few precious minutes, I realised I was being allowed to share her heart for strugglers and her passion for spiritual growth.

In contrast to today's plethora of connected devices, our family had a single computer at this time, a PC which we shared together and which Esther used to resolutely search the internet for opportunities that would stretch her walk with God. By the time we were allowed into the secret of what she was planning, her mind was made up. Youth With A Mission (affectionately known as "why-wham") offered a discipleship training scheme which sparked her enthusiasm.

"I like the look of this, Dad. I *really* like the look of it. They do six months of part training and part practice and you have to go to this really cool centre in the middle of nowhere. It looks like a country mansion and I'd get to live there. How cool is that!"

We had always encouraged Esther to spread her wings and find God's purpose for her life. As she stood in the impressive doorway of Holmsted Manor, a slip of a girl dwarfed by a

---

[1]   These are acronyms for Christian organisations which accept young people on mission projects.

mansion of a house, fatherly tenderness welled up within me. She seemed too small, too innocent to be facing this adventure, and my instinct to protect her would now have to give way to trusting God to look after her. She was taking flight.

The sleeping accommodation wasn't as cool as she first thought. Three beds could be fitted into the room where she was to sleep. In the bay window stood a battered 1950s dining-table that was to double as their shared desk. The beds however were bunks that had the appearance of being constructed from railway sleepers. Each bunk was three beds high. A threadbare sofa occupied the rest of the usable space between the bunks, which towered up towards the high ceiling.

The nine students who crammed into this room were from all over the world. Not only was Esther living away from home for the first time but she was also coming to terms with different accents, cultures and ways of living. She threw herself into the programme with gusto and her journal revealed meticulous notes on the teaching, along with revealing comments about the teachers:

> I thought there was a lot of depth to what D. was trying to communicate. Everything he said was also backed up with Bible references which is helpful. He also created enthusiasm for his next day of teaching.

> However he did at times speak too fast, making it hard to understand the point he was making. He also committed one of the most annoying and common teacher crimes which is to tell people to write something down and then continue teaching whilst they are doing it.

> However he is the best so far so all credit to him.

I'm not sure whether she realised the teacher would eventually see this comment, and when he did he added, "Oh Esther! You do make me laugh :)"

"So where's your mission trip going to be, then?" I asked as the second part of her programme was on the horizon. We expected to hear she was off to Balham or Bradford. Not for one moment did we expect Bolivia. YWAM had contacts with a rural church near La Paz, the capital, and they would be travelling on Christmas Eve with a stopover in Miami. While at the church they would be helping with a children's Bible club and teaching in the church.

Once in Bolivia, the sleeping arrangements were primitive in the extreme. The members of the team all slept together in the church sanctuary where only a rudimentary screen provided privacy. Each bed was made up of two pew-like benches turned inwards so the two seats were wide enough to accommodate a sleeping bag. But in the process of working out who was going to sleep where, they discovered there was one bench too few. Without a hint of complaining, Esther offered to sleep on this single remaining pew, and stayed there for several weeks so her teammates could enjoy wriggle room in their sleep.

"Dad, I've got to preach a sermon!" This time it was an e-mail from Bolivia. It continued: "and I need your help." I was flabbergasted. The idea of Esther preaching a sermon filled me with equal quantities of delight and astonishment. But rather than do only what she needed because it was expected of her, she launched into it with great enthusiasm. A flurry of e-mails bounced between us. "Dad, what does this verse really mean?..." "How on earth do I explain *that*?" "What do your notes look like when you preach? Can you send me some to look at?" Her preparation was meticulous. Verse by verse and story by story, her sermon began to take shape until the moment came for her to deliver it. She preached through an interpreter to an attentive Bolivian church.

"How did it go?" I asked in an e-mail.

"They listened, Dad – and they listened all the way through!" It's a shame e-mail can't convey tone of voice because I have a shrewd suspicion she was delighted with her ministry. Then in a rare moment of self-revelation she added, "Someone told me 'You don't say much, Esther, but what you say is deep. It's always worth hearing.'"

On reflection preaching was not quite so out of character as I might have supposed. A preacher is working from a set of ideas and usually a script. From the front of the church, she didn't need to respond to the unpredictability of conversational responses. So as long as she knew what she was going to say, this was a safe place for her to be. But we were increasingly learning that banter was moving off her personal agenda.

University

Rosi

Esther was always concerned that her life should count in a way that would benefit other people. She had little interest in purely theoretical subjects for which she could see no real life application. In the television programme that had originally sparked her imagination, the film maker had shown the work of a prosthetist as she painstakingly constructed artificial limbs. The victims of landmines in Cambodia and motorcycle accidents in Thailand, and diabetes sufferers in the UK, all had their lives transformed when they were fitted with customised prostheses. Here was a potential career that would combine her burgeoning love for science and make a difference to people.

So Esther started working on it, digging out as much as she could about courses, career opportunities and prospects, but all in the privacy of her own room. She was not going to be drawn on what she was up to until she had a plan. Gradually she became convinced this should be the focus of her life and began applying for university courses.

UCAS applications[1] are almost a rite of passage on their own. Work profiles, lists of achievements, exam grades and a welter of other information are poured out on to the forms. Most challenging of all, for most school-leavers, is the "personal statement", four thousand characters in which to describe your life, your personal vision and your aims. Esther beavered away on her own at her personal statement, and we were not allowed to see it until it was complete. She was going to assert her independence whatever the consequences. UCAS applications have space for five course choices with the student's first preference at number one. At great length she pored over her options and set her heart on studying at Strathclyde University in Glasgow.

So intensely focused was she that when it came to selecting a university, she only entered this single option on her application form. Despite it being so far from home, and being advised by her college that she would be wise to have a Plan B, she couldn't entertain the concept of alternatives.

"This is," she asserted, "God's plan for my life, so why bother with anything that's second best?"

Why indeed? But what would happen if she was rejected, or if her A-level results didn't match up? Surely it would be wise to

---

[1]   UCAS, the Universities and Colleges Admissions Service, is the central admissions scheme for UK universities.

have something in her back pocket in reserve? When we were alone, I approached it as delicately as I could:

"Have you thought of what you might do if Strathclyde don't offer you a place, dear?"

"I don't need a Plan B," was her retort; and with that the discussion was closed.

Ian

The transition to university was a huge step for Esther but her desire for independence was clearly a driving force in the decision. Glasgow is about a ten-hour drive from Eastbourne and we left as the sun rose with the car loaded to the gunnels with her belongings, including her well-loved red bicycle. The hall of residence was a functional grey-clad block of flats. Posters for discos, budget travel and yoga jostled for position on the meagre noticeboards, and small gruff placards warned of the dire consequences of sticking adverts anywhere else on the bright turquoise walls of the stairwells.

She climbed to the third floor and located her flat. She was to be sharing with five other students who could come from any part of the world. I watched her as she tried the key in the lock and gingerly pushed open the door to survey her new domain. It was a tiny rectangular box with a bed, a desk, a wardrobe and just enough room for a person to stand between them. So this was going to be her world for the next year.

Esther walked nervously into the communal kitchen and was met by another new student, also finding her way around.

"Hiya! And what's yourrr name?" the student asked, the long rolled "r" typical of a broad Scottish accent. Turning to see who was speaking to her, Esther came face to face with one of her new flatmates. She was shorter than Esther, very dark-skinned and beamed a huge welcoming smile. Somehow her accent seemed incongruous for someone sporting such intricately woven dreadlocks. To Esther's delight, Annette turned out to be the daughter of a Pentecostal pastor from the north of Scotland, and was herself an enthusiastic Christian. It was not long before they were deep in conversation, comparing notes about journeys, prospects and churches.

Esther soon became devoted to her studies. The combination of engineering and medicine seemed to chime with her preferences and she felt God had taken her to the right place. She would often ring home for a mathematical consultation with her Dad, and gave herself wholeheartedly to her academic work. Usually alone.

By the time her second year started, the dual tasks of building relationships and managing the work were becoming stressful for her (and we began to see some evidence of strain in her life). She began to develop a strategy of being tightly programmed to enable her to cope. Lists for work, lists for chores, lists for her spiritual life, all adorned her walls. Soon we began to notice how exhausted she was when she came home for holidays. We did our best to provide what she needed – extensive time and space to recover and regain her mental and physical energy for the return. But in spite of its opportunities, university was taking its toll.

Releasing the word

Ian

After exploring several churches in Glasgow, Esther settled on St George's Tron which had a highly organised ministry to students. She often said that the highlight of her week was Thursday evening when she came to a meeting entitled "Release the Word". Here students would eat, hear a talk and discuss the Bible together, and it was in this enquiring atmosphere that her understanding of the Bible was stimulated to a greater depth. It often prompted a phone call home to consult me again – this time about theology – and it was clear that her faith was growing rapidly. Other people noticed this too and they would often say of her that she listened with rapt attention and, although she said very little, when she opened her mouth there was always depth and thoughtfulness in her contribution.

Her love for the Bible and for God grew enormously through Release the Word. After she died, one of her friends said:

> I loved chatting with Esther. There seemed a whole world of thought beneath. The more I learn about Esther the more I'm convinced she was an uncommon woman with such a unique, almost indescribable experience of the Lord.

And that wasn't all. On a Facebook group about Esther after she died, a friend of hers wrote:

> God has taught us so much through Esther's life and how her relationship with Him was everything to her! Awesome!

Odd

Rosi

In spite of her shyness, Esther was far from humourless and was quite capable of observing the odd, the comical or the strangely twisted. Even when at school, she could come up with gems that had been carefully thought out before they would ever leave her lips. The end of the final term at school gave each of the students a chance to write a single sentence of greeting for all the other students in the class. These would be printed in a special book to be given to the school leavers.

While other members of the class had used their space to proclaim the likes of: "Have a nice life" or "Dave will always be remembered for his bear hugs ... arrrrh!" or "I had a good time at school but I'm glad I'm leaving", Esther had to make her contribution less trivial. Beneath a modest photograph of her in school uniform was the tantalising inscription:

> I was going to leave an empty space to create an air of mystery, but there wasn't enough room.

Esther could be hilariously funny. A single comment or apparently chance remark could reduce people to fits of laughter, and there were many times when her astute observations about people were packaged in sharp wit. When she felt secure, there was a carefree quality to Esther's conversation that endeared her to the people in her world. "She was often quiet and reserved especially around large groups or unfamiliar faces," said one of her friends, "but then she would suddenly come out with these real gems and observations that would make me laugh till I ached!"

Her childlike quirkiness never left her and when we asked her how she would like to celebrate her twenty-first birthday, she proclaimed without a moment's hesitation, "Tandems. I want us to ride tandems. And I want to cycle with Dad, Mum, Chris and Polly in Scotland." The trip was promptly arranged.

While Esther was a delightful person to be with at times like these, there were forces within her that were beginning to concern us. When we congratulated her for some achievement or showed our love for her, she didn't seem to know how to respond. Her life was increasingly dominated by lists of what to do and when to do it and the chaos in her living space, once an endearing quirk, was now becoming a liability. Esther's expressions of delight, love or joy, once so much a natural part of our lives, were becoming less frequent. Indeed, in our darker moments, we wondered if we'd done something terribly wrong. Ian wrote her a special letter for her twenty-first because we wanted her to be sure about the special place she held in our lives. If she was finding it increasingly difficult to express or even comprehend love, we wanted her to be sure that it would always be extended to her. Here is what Ian said:

Dear Esther

I want to write to you for your twenty-first birthday because there are some things on my heart that I want to share with you at such a significant milestone in your life.

Quite honestly I can hardly comprehend that is was twenty-one years ago that God gave you to us as it still feels as if it happened only a few months ago! What is more, although you may not realise it, the fact that you were born on 31st May, the same day that I was born again some years earlier, has always made you very precious to me.

A few months later when you were dedicated I adapted a hymn for us to sing at the service. It reflected our desires and prayers for you from the very earliest moments of your life and it runs like this.[1]

Since then Mum and I have been overjoyed to see how God has answered this prayer in your life. Your kindness, your faithfulness, your determination and your faith have all been an example to us. We love you and we're proud of you – and we're proud, not only of your achievements, but of the person you are.

I am all too aware that on occasions I have been far from a perfect father and haven't reflected the perfect

---

[1]   This is the hymn we refer to in chapter 3

fatherhood that God models for us. For those moments I need your forgiveness and God's grace.

So on your twenty-first birthday Mum and I want you to know that you are one of the best things that ever happened in our lives. And as you face a promising future in a turbulent world we want you to know that whether you meet with success or tragedy, whether you end up being rich or poor – even whether you choose to follow God or reject Him – we will always love you and stand with you because nothing can change the precious fact that you are our daughter.

I love you.

Dad

We watched as she read it intently then put it back in its envelope without a word.

Dress code

Ian

As an adult Esther's default dress code was jeans and a fleece and this self-effacing clothing defined her appearance. In common with her speaking, where she would be reserved but capable of sudden voluble outbursts, so she was in her dress. Her conservatism could be suddenly broken by, for example, dressing as a human penguin to win a fancy dress competition. She went on to surprise everyone by looking elegant and glamorous in a purple bridesmaid dress at her brother's wedding. It was clear, however, that the attention her elegance aroused was unsettling, and as soon as the celebrations were over it was back to the jeans and fleece. To our knowledge she never wore the dress again.

The Road Not Chosen

As we left Glasgow after her twenty-first birthday, our minds were filled with images of near misses on the bikes, hilarity over our picnics and the sense of privilege at sharing one of life's milestones with her. But something unnerving was happening. She seemed to be retreating more often into a world of her own from which even some of the people closest to her were excluded. Our phone calls, once full of excited chatter, would now contain (sometimes very long) pauses. In conversation, she would occasionally go completely silent.

I noticed it as a father in the way she greeted me when coming home from a trip or arriving in the airport. Gone was throwing her arms round Dad, and instead she would nervously give me an A-frame hug involving the minimum of human contact. Conversation was becoming awkward too, with Esther at times not engaging with us in moments where previously words would have flowed. We noticed that birthday and Christmas cards had a different autograph. No longer were they signed off with "Loads of love from Esther" followed by a row of kisses; we just saw "From Esther". Rosi and I would mull over this deep into the night without coming to a resolution.

When she came home, Esther would retreat into her darkened bedroom to sit for hours on end, absorbed in her own thoughts. Many older teens and early twenties use their parents' house like a hotel and we were quite content with her desiring solitude, but this was different. If I came into a room where she was sitting, she would quietly stand up and go to another. There was something making her keep her distance from people in her world, even some of us very close to her. In my private thoughts, I ruminated on whether something in my parenting had gone so drastically awry that she no longer wanted to identify with us.

And occasionally there would be a meltdown. Usually triggered by an insignificant disagreement or divergence of opinion, Esther could fly off the handle and there seemed nothing we could say or do to pacify her. Seeing her barge out of the back door, try to engage me in a fight and then run out into the street was deeply worrying. For most of that evening and into the night she was absent. I drove round the streets to see if I could find her, and when she came into view, walking as if on a route march, she wouldn't get into the car. We were on the verge of calling the police when she returned home, let herself in silently, and went to her darkened bedroom. In the morning it was as if it had never happened, and however gently we broached the subject to resolve outstanding tension, it was a closed book. All families have their tensions and ours is no exception, but this was so far out of character that first of all we debated whether we had done something to upset her so gravely or, as we have said previously, whether there was a change going on within.

Complexity

Ian and Rosi

You will have sensed from this overview of Esther's life that as parents we faced some dilemmas about her. The bright personality she showed as a child was being overshadowed by forces with altogether darker strands. This complexity in her character raised deep questions in our minds for which we still don't have many answers. Living with this uncertainty has been something we have had to get used to as we have grieved her loss.

Hindsight can be a devastating thing and it is easy for us to denigrate ourselves by saying "If only we'd noticed this at the time!" But we try to avoid this if we can. Parenting is one of the greatest privileges life can offer, but it can also be unpredictable.

8

Pain, the Uninvited Guest

Lord, help us to accept the pains and conflicts that
come to us each day as opportunities to grow as
people and become more like you. (Mother Teresa)

When you pass through the waters,
I will be with you;
when you pass through the rivers,
they will not sweep over you;
when you walk through the fire,
you will not be burned ...
for I am the Lord your God ...
You are precious and honoured in my sight,
and I love you.
(Isaiah 43:2-4 paraphrase)

Ian and Rosi

Christmas was coming and we were looking forward to seeing Esther again. Our trips to the airport always filled us with anticipation and there was excited chatter between us as we set off for Gatwick. Once in the clinical atmosphere of the terminal, we were ready to play the game of who's-going-to-see-her-first as the flight's passengers emerged from the arrivals tunnel. We waited. By now the whole flight had disembarked and dissipated into the airport terminal with no sign of Esther. A minute or so later the entrance to the tunnel slowly opened again as Esther leaned her back against the door, pushing with all her might and dragging her rucksack behind her.

She smiled at us in greeting but it was a weary smile that carried as much relief as it did joy at seeing us. There was something very different about the Esther who had just forced her way through that door. Her face was gaunt and her movements stiff. Instead of running to meet us she plodded, with every step an effort.

Rosi leaned over and whispered, "She looks shattered."

Instead of striding along with her bag slung over her back, she held it by her side, swapping hands twice in the few paces before we met. Her jaw protruded and her eyes seemed slightly sunken. As she came closer, we noticed her fingers were angular. She plonked her bag on the floor and gave us powerless hugs. Drawing a long, deep breath, she said, "Can you carry my bag for me, Dad?"

We could barely hear her. Her normally clear voice was gruff and weak and her legs had puppet-like movements. We knew she'd had a tiring term but something had knocked the stuffing out of her and we glanced concern towards each other. As we began talking, it soon became clear that things had changed. Her breathing was laboured. Over the previous few weeks, Rosi had become concerned that Esther sounded more tired than usual but there had been a step change in her exhaustion.

"I haven't been feeling well actually," she confided in the car. "It's since we did the bag stunt that I've been a bit off-colour."

"Tell us about this 'bag stunt' then."

"Some of my year group are hoping to go to Cambodia so we had this idea. If we go to Morrisons we could pack people's bags and ask them for a donation. The manager was cool with it so we did it for a whole day!"

"So you've been standing all day in a supermarket packing bags, eh?"

"Yep – but we raised lots of money for the trip to Cambodia."

"No wonder you're tired."

"It was good fun, though." And with that she dozed off on the back seat.

As we drove we both knew that a single day as a bag lady could never produce this level of exhaustion. Something else was taking its toll.

Hospitalisation

Ian

Esther's condition did not improve. She was lethargic and her breathing was increasingly laboured. The rasping quality of her voice did not go away with a night's sleep, and the next morning her temperature began to rise. Paracetamol treatment did not appear to ease her condition.

Grace, my mother, was staying with us for the Christmas break. We had brought her to Eastbourne from her care home to have a few days by the sea and to be part of the family's celebrations. She appeared in the kitchen in dressing-gown and slippers.

"Can I help you to get breakfast ready?" she asked.

"If you like, how about setting the table?"

"Where are your knives and spoons, then?"

"In that drawer there." I pointed and she rummaged.

Five minutes of counting, thinking, arranging and rearranging took place before she was satisfied she'd found the right collection of cutlery. It was now in a disordered pile on the table with Grace looking at it, dithering.

"Can I help you with that, Grandma?" Esther's uncharacteristically gruff voice came from the doorway.

"Of course darling. I'm just not sure ..." And in an instant Esther came to Grace's rescue, lovingly working with her to set the table and avoid further embarrassment.

When Grace was out of the room, Esther sidled up to me with a wry smile. "So this morning I'm granny-sitting, am I?"

"In a manner of speaking, yes, but if there's a problem, just let me know," I responded. "I'll only be round the corner in the church."

Grace had always had an affinity with Esther ever since she was a baby, and they enjoyed each other's company. But Grace was becoming more forgetful, and to have another adult in the house was a wise precaution. It was Christmas Eve, and Rosi and I both had deadlines to meet at work. In truth, we were also anxious and Rosi rang in the middle of the morning to see how things were. When Esther answered the phone, her voice was so weak she could barely be heard and it was clear that something was seriously wrong. Rosi rang me in the church. "You need to go home now, darling, Esther needs some help urgently."

It was not what I wanted to hear. When I arrived, Esther was breathing heavily and only able to speak in a whisper. The sight of her slender body slouched on a sofa and her rasping voice made me shudder. Our local clinic was only a few streets away and I was able to book in with them for a few hours later. But when the time came to go to the surgery, Esther could barely stand.

"Get the office chair from my bedroom," she commanded.

"Why on earth do you want that?" I asked. "We need to go to the doctor's." But she was not going to enter into discussion.

"Just get it," she insisted, and I obediently went upstairs to her bedroom to retrieve the small blue swivel chair she used at her desk. It had five wheels. As soon as I brought it to her, she hauled herself out of the sofa and flopped like a rag doll on the chair.

"Now push me to the car," she whispered.

At once I could see her plan. So powerless was she that her desk chair would make do as a wheelchair. Once in the clinic, her breathing difficulties worsened and we were ushered past the waiting patients, straight into the surgery. I sat on the far side of the room while the GP examined her. With a tender voice he probed her condition, but when he started to take her blood pressure, we both had a surprise. As her sleeve was rolled up, it became clear that Esther's arm was far too thin for the cuff to fit. He shot a look of concern in my direction.

"Is Esther usually this thin?" he said.

"Oh, our super-fit daughter's always been slim," I quipped. But as I looked on at the doctor attempting to take a blood pressure reading, it was clear Esther had lost more weight than any of us realised. He was concerned, so was I, and we both knew that her weight was now an elephant in the room.

It was clear her condition was worsening even while we were sitting there. Diagnosing pneumonia, the doctor said, "We have two options, Mr White. Either you drive her to Hastings where I know there is a bed, or I call an ambulance and we take her to the local A&E."

This was a heart-rending dilemma. The road between Eastbourne and Hastings is notoriously prone to blockages and I genuinely didn't want to prolong Esther's discomfort by making the journey. But there was no certainty of a bed at the local hospital. Seeing her distress, we opted for the ambulance, and within minutes paramedics had carried her on a stretcher chair into the waiting ambulance. Once inside they strapped an oxygen mask on her pallid face. Events were now taking place at breathtaking speed and I rang Rosi to tell her to meet me at the hospital.

Esther and I were separated for a few minutes while I gave the receptionist her details. A doctor who had been examining her confirmed pneumonia and spoke blithely about "popping her into resuss". Resuss? What was she being resuscitated from? At this moment Rosi arrived and we could both see how seriously ill Esther had become.

Rosi

I felt a sense of helplessness. Seeing Esther lying there suffering so much more than she had been, only a few hours before, was profoundly shocking. Ian and I were ushered into the waiting area, and after what seemed an eternity, the ward sister came to talk with us. Turning a spare chair to face our direction, she got the pleasantries out of the way before adopting an earnest tone.

"Did Esther have breakfast this morning?"

"Yes, she ate it with the family."

"Did she have a meal last night?"

Pain, the Uninvited Guest

"Yes, she'd just come off a flight from Glasgow where she's studying and we all had dinner together. She was hungry!"

"What is her appetite like, normally?"

"Pretty good. She may be slim, but she can pack away a good meal. And she has a passion for authentic curries with all the original spices. They're gorgeous and she'll make them for all of us sometimes."

I couldn't figure out where this line of questioning might be leading us.

"Why d'you ask?" I enquired. "This doesn't seem to have much to do with pneumonia."

"I helped to undress her," she replied, "and noticed how exceptionally thin she was. We may be looking at anorexia."

This was a bombshell we did not expect and my mind began running down uncomfortable burrows, each one more disturbing than the last. "How come we never noticed?" "Why was this happening and why did Esther not give the slightest hint of it?" "How does this reflect on us as parents that she could be so disturbed within herself and we didn't realise?" "How on earth did we not spot she wasn't eating?" But she was. The evidence just didn't fit.

We went into her cubicle and sat by her bed. Tubes and wires snaked in all directions and the gentle whirrs and bleeps of machinery provided our background music. After a few minutes a cheery doctor breezed in to see her. He talked with her briefly without a response, checked some readings and pulled up a chair on the opposite side of her bed.

The Road Not Chosen

"Well," he said, as if about to make a pronouncement. "Esther is deep in ketoacidosis[1] and we think we can pull her through. It will be an uncomfortable twenty-four hours and she'll need to be on insulin for the rest of her life. But she's lucky. Fifty years ago she would have been dead."

I wanted to take him on one side and give him a good talking to. Someone, somewhere, has got to tell him he has the bedside manner of a mallet.

For the rest of that day and into Christmas Day, Esther was obviously in pain. Although every breath was laced with oxygen, each one was a Herculean effort, and as she lay under observation, we felt a curious mixture of gratitude that she had been spared and foreboding over what the future might hold. Diabetes was new territory for all of us. Curiously we felt relieved that anorexia had not been the cause of her weight loss, but we were only just beginning to realise the implications of Esther living with Type 1 diabetes.

Ian

Christmas Day came and we were both heavily committed to the celebrations at the church – one of the most important in the calendar. The church was packed with regular members, guests and visitors from all over the country. Children had brought presents to show off and there was an air of joyful exuberance throughout the auditorium. Majestic Christmas carols, dramatic Bible passages and gales of laughter filled the air. I found myself preaching on autopilot. My body was in the church, my notes were on the lectern and my images were on the giant screen, but my heart was in the hospital. We had told

---

[1] Ketoacidosis is a pathological metabolic state marked by an extreme accumulation of keto acids. Amongst other consequences this causes the blood to become more acidic and in extreme cases ketoacidosis can be fatal.

a few close friends who had promised to pray, and we now knew we were going to need their support to see this through. We left the church as quickly as decency would allow and sat at Esther's bedside, feeding her jelly for her Christmas dinner.

She spent four nights in hospital and showed little emotional reaction to her circumstances. As a family, we had always been quite open about our feelings, so Esther's locking down of her emotions was a departure that mystified us. Chris and Polly dropped everything to travel to see her and succeeded in making her smile. But it was an exception.

"Is it just me," I confided to Rosi, "or does she come over as sort of flat? Emotionally, I mean."

"No, dear, it's not just you. She's been behaving a bit oddly recently and this kind of trauma really isn't going to help. She's kind, generous, helpful and all that, but where have the hugs gone?"

We both felt concern over how emotionally monotone Esther had become. If she was carrying some burden on the private side of her life, a traumatic diagnosis would only add to her difficulty. Would she cope with a radically changed lifestyle?

When she was discharged, she was very relieved to be out of hospital, and commented that she was pleased she'd been hospitalised at home in Eastbourne and not in Scotland. But she hardly spoke about it at all and when we asked how she was or how she felt, she would dodge the question or simply not respond. We were never quite sure whether she was unable to talk about it, or whether her diabetes was something she wanted to manage herself on the private side of life. It quickly emerged that, diabetes or no, she was doggedly determined to return to university as quickly as she could, ignoring all the advice to take life easy for a week or two. By this time we were very concerned she hadn't recovered enough. Maybe she was finding it difficult to be the focus of attention and, although she did delay returning, it was only by a single day.

Our feelings at this point were a strange mixture of concern and relief. We were thinking, "Lots of people have diabetes and most of them manage it well, so why shouldn't Esther? She's intelligent, she's self-disciplined and, although it will be a burden she will carry lifelong, her determination and her faith will help to see her through." But we remained apprehensive.

Easter

Ian and Rosi

Back in Scotland, Esther took her exams and passed them comfortably. Appointments with the Royal Infirmary were happening and we were given to understand her diabetes was getting under control. So far as we were aware, she was adjusting to her new situation as well as could be expected. So when Rosi went to visit her she was relieved to find Esther healthier. Our daily phone calls seemed to confirm this. Easter was coming and the university semester spanned the holiday weekend so she would have to stay in Glasgow to complete her assignments.

It was Maundy Thursday and Esther had rung at about 11pm for her nightly update. Nothing unusual had happened, she'd done some washing, done some work, cooked herself a meal and all seemed well.

"Noisy line, though," Rosi observed.

At midnight we were drifting into sleep when there was an insistent ringing on our bell. Midnight pastoral crises do happen but they are rare. So we scurried downstairs in our nightclothes to unbolt and open the door. There, a little bedraggled but with a beaming smile across her face, stood Esther.

"Hellooo," she intoned.

We were speechless.

"W-what a wonderful surprise! You've just flown down from Glasgow!"

"Yep."

"So where were you when you rang just now?"

"On the train, where d'you think?"

"So that's the noise I could hear in the background – and you walked all the way from the station!"

"Yep."

The daughter who had just arrived looked completely different from the one who left at Christmas. By this time she had gained weight and her jeans were now supporting a muffin top. Esther certainly knew how to spring a surprise, and the thrill of having her in the home over the celebration added an extra layer of joy. It wasn't long, however, before our concerns over her health began to grow again. Any attempt, however gentle or indirect, to talk about it resulted in a firmly closed door. Her health was a no-go area in conversation and we sensed a "Parents Keep Out" notice on the whole topic. What we didn't know at the time was that everybody had to keep out. Even the medics.

Crisis

Rosi

We both felt it was important to listen to what God was saying about Esther. Sometimes we write down our prayer-impressions of His messages for us, and I wrote this in my journal as a word from the Lord: "I know you are burdened about Esther. I love her and have a plan for her life. I ask you to love her and pray for her, trusting Me to work in her life. She is very precious to Me and to you and I have a surprising plan for her which will gradually be revealed." In our own praying, this idea that God was going to do something surprising in her was becoming a recurring theme.

Esther's cousin Lizzie was to be married and our whole family had been invited to the celebrations in Banstead, Surrey. I spoke to Esther to confirm her flight arrangements for the Friday evening.

"It's weird, Mum," she said. "I slept for eighteen hours non-stop and I still feel drowsy."

We were worried. As we were preparing to leave Eastbourne to collect Esther from the airport, the phone went again. This time it was Esther's friend, Chloe.

"We're ringing about Esther," she said. Her voice sounded troubled. "We haven't seen her all day and decided to check her room. A few minutes ago we found her lying semi-conscious on the floor."

There's a sinking feeling that comes with news like this. The distance, the unknowing and the helplessness all became mixed together as our minds tried to process what we were hearing.

Pain, the Uninvited Guest

"We've called the paramedics and they're working on her now but I don't think she'll be travelling."

What an understatement! An hour later Chloe rang again.

"Esther has come round and is talking to us now but she's not letting them take her to the hospital."

"Could I talk with her please?" I asked and found myself speaking to Esther. No matter how sensitively I broached the subject, any talk about her condition, of hospital or of medical care was met with a closed door. She didn't give me the impression I was intruding; it appeared to be something she just couldn't face.

"I'm OK Mum," she insisted, "and I'm not on my own."

"But don't you think it might be helpful to at least let them check you over, dear?"

"That's not going to happen, Mum."

Silence.

By Saturday morning Esther was in hospital. Her flatmates had persuaded her to go, and clubbed together to pay for the taxi to get her there. Somehow the fear of seeing the medics was becoming greater than the danger and discomfort of the disease itself, so all we could do was to pray. As we travelled to our niece's wedding, we remained troubled.

"I can't get my head round this," Ian sighed at the wheel. "She has Type 1 and doesn't want to talk to us about it. Fair enough. Although I'm sure we'd have been able to have *some* sort of conversation about it in years past."

The car pulled up in a queue at traffic lights and Ian turned to face me. "I'm really worried, darling."

"So am I, and it's not just the diabetes Ian, it's the not talking about it that worries me more. It's not Esther."

The traffic lights changed and Ian, distracted, lurched the car into motion.

"Ooops. Sorry. Not thinking."

"Our minds are both somewhere else," I mused. "Can I ask you something?"

He nodded.

"Ian, I can't get it out of my mind, but what would have happened if Chloe hadn't checked on her?"

"I know. That thought's been going round in my head too. It doesn't bear thinking about, does it?"

We travelled on to the wedding to the sound of Radio 4. We listened to the whole programme but heard none of it.

Ian

The big family wedding was a blur. I was preaching to a full church at the service and fortunately had prepared very thoroughly. I was preaching once more on autopilot, constantly thinking of Esther in Glasgow. I knew Rosi felt guilty about even being at the wedding but relieved that Esther was safe in hospital. We tried to renegotiate flights so that Rosi could travel to Glasgow on the ticket we had already purchased for Esther's return, but it proved impossible to contact the airline on the phone at the weekend. In our worry about Esther, the minor frustration of not being able to transfer a flight assumed a size out of all proportion to its significance. I'm sure the meal was delicious; I honestly don't remember.

Pain, the Uninvited Guest

Rosi

The Sunday flight was the first ticket I could buy, so I flew to Glasgow and found my way to the sprawling hospital. I raced through the interminable corridors to locate the diabetic ward. There I found Esther along with a collection of comatose octogenarians.

"Hello Mum," Esther said flatly when she saw me, and did her best to give me a hug.

"How are you feeling, dear?" I asked.

"I'm OK. My brain feels addled, but I'm OK."

"Can you tell me what happened?"

Silence.

"It's lovely to see you."

"You too, Mum."

Silence.

"Have the nurses talked to you about how you are?"

Silence.

"Dad sends lots of love to you."

Silence.

Mystification coupled with a tinge of anger began to rise within me. Why wouldn't she talk to me? Why wouldn't she even respond to simple factual enquiries? Why wouldn't she even tell me what had happened? Increasingly anguished, I wondered why we didn't seem to be able to connect like we used to. Where had all the banter gone? Then, as if in a moment of disturbing clarity, I began to see something altogether darker. Maybe it was not true that she wouldn't talk.

Maybe she couldn't.

It was a Bank Holiday weekend and the medical oversight was severely stretched. My anxiety grew as I became more aware of her pain and turmoil. She had become withdrawn and distant. With gentle encouragement, Esther did tell me that she had been talking to her course tutor about only taking some of her exams in the summer. Then in a rare moment of openness, she said, "It's funny, Mum. I feel like I'm a spectator on my life and my brain feels addled all the time."

She went on to say she thought a physical imbalance in her brain was its cause rather than anything emotional or psychological. Esther was aware she had a problem with communication and she wanted to find some help to resolve it.

"Would you let me talk with the consultant when he comes?" I asked her. There was some reluctance on her part but she gave me the nod. When the consultant came, each new fact that emerged compounded my anxiety.

"Now I can tell you what happened," he continued. "Esther came in with an excess of insulin in her blood, and since her pancreas is no longer operating effectively, this must have been self-administered. It's the only way it could have got into her system."

"Are you telling me this could have been deliberate?"

"Who knows? But we'd like to do a psychiatric assessment, just to be on the safe side ... if she will agree."

In my hurry I hadn't booked a hotel, and found myself sleeping in Esther's own student room. Being in her house, I was able to chat with her housemates and was genuinely touched by their concern for me. They shared my anxiety and reassured me that Esther did have supportive friends around her. But being among them, watching them get on with the ordinary stuff of university life, only emphasised the gulf between their ability to cope and Esther's.

"She seems confused at times," they told me, "and she's obviously struggling with everyday activities. Money, clothes, work, you name it and she's in a muddle somewhere. She does play the piano beautifully, though. The only way Esther seems to manage is by writing lists. Loads of them."

Each night as I climbed into my daughter's bed, I was confronted with her turmoil. Even by Esther's slightly muddly standard, her room was exceptionally chaotic and the other girls had even washed her clothes for her.

I felt alone. I was alone. The usual sources of support like Ian were hundreds of miles away and all I could do was to hang on to the assurances that people were praying for me. Then, as if to say "I haven't forgotten you", God sent Agnes across my path. Agnes, as we have said, was the pastor for students at Esther's church, affectionately called "The Tron", and she brought a ray of hope into my situation. She came to visit every day. Her faith-filled caring, which went way beyond the call of duty, helped keep my head above water and assured me that the isolation I felt was not complete. We would talk about the events of the day and the health of Esther and she would say, "Shall we pray now?" Then for the following few minutes, in a gentle voice, she would talk to God about each of the things we'd shared. Together we called on His strength to see us through even if we didn't feel it at the time. In the Bible there is a promise God gives to His people to claim when they are in distress: "When you pass through the waters, I will be with you." (Isaiah 43:2 which we put at the head of this chapter.) And Agnes was God's way of showing it to me.

The Road Not Chosen

Partly to keep the university abreast of developments and partly to enquire how Esther was doing, I went with Esther's permission to visit her tutor. It soon became clear that her condition was affecting her work in ways I had not imagined. Although she was coping with the written work, Esther appeared at times to be in a diabetic daze which affected her relationships at every turn. She was finding it difficult to communicate with patients and this threatened to prevent her progressing to the clinical placement part of her course. Her tutor suggested that she didn't take any of her exams at this point and considered whether a different course might be more appropriate for her. I wondered how many more knocks Esther could take? Her health, her fitness, and now her prospects, were all in jeopardy. I could only speculate as to what was going on inside my daughter who kept so many of her thoughts to herself.

I now became vividly aware of how passionately Esther wanted to complete her course. Quitting was not going to be part of her vocabulary, and although I assured her that all was not lost and that we have a loving God who can guide us into good plans that are His best for us, she saw any suggestion of giving up as betrayal. When I went back to see her she was downcast, concluding (falsely) that her tutor had lost faith in her. Reluctantly she agreed not to take her exams and to see the psychiatrist.

Talking to the psychiatrist seemed to have helped Esther, and when I spoke to him (again with her permission) he confirmed that she did not score highly for depression but her difficulties were more akin to an intense social anxiety disorder or possibly Asperger's Syndrome. I was relieved to hear he felt he could help her as this might have gone some way to explaining the more disquieting aspects of her relationship with us. So far as Esther herself was concerned, her confusion was a physical not a psychological thing, but she did agree she could benefit from some help with her communication.

I can honestly describe this as one of the worst weeks of my life. Miles away from home with my daughter in such personal pain, I couldn't see how it would end. It was a sweltering hot Glasgow day and I walked to the river, flopped on a bench and rang Ian. When he answered, I just wept down the phone to him.

"What can we do?" I sobbed. "Esther is in hospital, the university say she probably won't be able to complete her course, she's being seen by a psych and she hardly speaks! What can we do? What *can* we do?"

Although tender, Ian felt as powerless as I did, except to promise that he and others would pray. I didn't doubt that God cared about Esther but I was mystified by how His sovereignty was going to work out in her body or her mind. Prayers may not always be answered by miracles but the compassion they show gave me some reassurance.

9

Cambodia

Ian and Rosi

Esther had, by now, missed part of her course and questions were already in the air about whether the university would allow her to complete it.

"But I can't give up!" she said, her voice full of urgency. "I just can't. Quitting isn't going to happen, especially now I've done so much work for our trip."

The question of whether it would be wise, or even possible, for her to go on the group's field trip to Cambodia now raised its head. Esther went to see her doctor alone, and that single act put us on the horns of a dilemma. On the one hand, she was having so much difficulty in communicating that she might not be able to take part in the conversation, let alone bring herself to ask questions. At the same time we both wanted her to be as independent as she could. Although our child was an adult we still felt responsible, even though many channels of communication were closed to us.

So concerned were we that the medics were not hearing the whole story, that we wrote a detailed letter to the psychiatrist. He would be unaware of information we had at our fingertips. So we shared it all with him: home life, student life and the huge changes in concentration and motivation we were seeing as parents. That, however, was really the end of our meaningful contact with professionals, as Esther wanted to handle things by herself from then on, come what may. So this was the dilemma: our hearts went out to her but we were being excluded from the very channels of communication that could potentially help her. Respecting her independence and trusting her to God were all we could do from now on.

Rosi

"How are the preparations for Cambodia going?" I asked on the phone one night.

"Oh, OK," she said. "I've got my rucksack and I've got £40 out of the cash point. It seems a lot of money, do you think it'll be enough?"

"Darling, it will be a bit like Bolivia. You won't be able to use sterling so you'll need to think of getting some local currency. Out in the sticks there's no guarantee you'll be able to use your debit card either. What are the others doing?"

"I don't know Mum. They all seem to have got everything sorted already and I'm ...." She paused as if she'd hit the buffers.

"Oh Esther!" My heart went out to her. "I know you'd rather I didn't ask but I'm sure the airline won't let you on board without a letter to say you need to carry your needles. Have you been given one yet?"

"Um, I don't think I've got one."

"And medical insurance?" On the other end of the line there was a shuffling of papers. "I don't expect the university will be happy about you going without any insurance."

Cambodia

"Um, I don't know. I'll have to ask."

"OK, can we do this together? Why don't you organise an 'I'm-diabetic-and-need-my-needles' type of letter and we'll investigate travel insurance when you've found out if the university will cover you. Will that help?"

"Yes Mum. Thanks."

Ian

It was heart-rending to look on as Esther became more befuddled over things she would once have taken in her stride. In fact she was finding it more and more difficult to organise some of the basics of life. The trip to Cambodia did require her to carry adequate personal health insurance, and a phone call revealed her difficulty.

"Dad, they won't let me go without health insurance and I don't know what to do. You get your own insurance when you travel, don't you? Can you help me?"

"I'll try, but why are they turning you down?"

"Dunno. They keep asking questions about me and then say no. I so desperately want to go to Cambodia."

"I know you do, dear. There is an insurance broker I use sometimes who might be able to help. I'll give him a ring."

When I phoned, the news was no more encouraging. No matter which providers the broker tried, Esther's health history was against her. So realising that her prospects lay in my hands, I made it my mission to find some cover for her. Scouring the internet for every reputable insurance company I could find, I spent most of my non-work time trying to track down anyone who might offer her some level of protection. Every time it was the same story.

"I'm sorry sir. As there have been two hospital admissions within the last six months and a history of diabetes, we can't offer you cover." It was starting to sound like a mantra and I would have to break the news to her.

"Esther, I've got some sad news for you, and there's no easy way to tell you, but I've not been able to find you any insurance. I'm terribly sorry, I've really given it my best shot." I longed to be able to comfort her and empathise with her but she was completely silent. I feared she might hold us responsible for her having to stay in the UK while her university friends were abroad.

Love

Ian

At this point I took a decision. It is hard to describe what it feels like as a father when your daughter's communication becomes increasingly factual and detached. Phone conversations would contain long pauses as she consciously struggled to work out what she should say. So I created a Facebook account so we could try communicating on screen which Esther seemed to find easier. I would look forward to hearing the Facebook "poke" ping from my PC's speakers.

"How R U Dad? what U doing?" Our conversation would flow better in text than it did on the phone. Sometimes she found her old sense of humour and would chide me for having so few friends on Facebook: my one compared with her twenty-five.

What concerned me was her increasing inability to respond to emotions, words of affirmation and expressions of love. Not just mine, but anybody's, it seemed. Even birthday cards were autographed with just "Esther" in contrast to her childhood expressions of love, devotion, poems and kisses. I had no doubt in my own heart that Esther loved us dearly but it seemed as if her emotional capacity was becoming more intensely locked down as the weeks went on. So I made a resolution that each time I spoke to Esther on the phone, I would tell her in some suitable way that I loved her. I wouldn't tell her that she was loved (that's passive) or that we loved her (that's plural) but that I loved her. Sometimes it was a simple sign-off, "I love you dear – bye!" At other times I'd expand a bit.

I will never know how she received her father's love but I desperately wanted her to know that it was there, it was real, it was constant and it was unconditional.

God's fingerprints

Ian

Not long afterwards, Esther made a trip to chill out with Chris and Polly in Cheltenham. Esther's relationship with Rosi and me had become a little strained, partly (we surmise) because we'd been the bearers of so much bad news. So we were relieved to know she was with her brother and enjoying herself. Then this happened:

"Dad!" She sounded excited, even ebullient, for the first time in months. "I'm going to Cambodia!"

"Really? How did that come about?"

"Chris and I trawled the internet. We sat down and wouldn't get up until we found some insurance. And we found it! And I'm going to Cambodia!"

"Esther, that's great to hear, I'm so pleased."

The Road Not Chosen

Was I? In truth I felt a mixture of anxiety that she might have thought we had tried to obstruct her, and concern that the policy was genuinely adequate, given the fragility of her health. But what could we do apart from assure her we'd support her in the venture and keep our concerns to ourselves? So our responsibility now was to find a way of dealing with our own anxiety without letting on to Esther. We prayed, once again committing her future into God's hands.

"Ian." Rosi's brow was furrowed as she looked up when we'd finished praying. "Whenever I pray for Esther, I get the sense that the Lord is going to do something surprising in her life. Maybe this is going to be part of it."

"Maybe."

Rosi

Reassurance that God was on her case was to come from an unexpected source. It was Saturday 31st May, Esther's twenty-second birthday, when the phone rang.

"Hi Ros, it's Susie here." Susie was a born enthusiast for God, and hearing her voice filled me with anticipation.

"Just ringing for a catch-up," she went on. "We feel you could do with some prayer at the moment but I guess that's an understatement! Anyway, how are you two doing these days?"

I spent the next few minutes retelling our story and spilling out my concern over Esther's visit to Cambodia. Susie listened empathetically and then broke into my flow.

"That's extraordinary!" she exclaimed. "Several months ago I had a strong sensation that God was telling me to write 'Cambodia' in my prayer diary for May 31st. I had no idea why at the time. I just knew that something connected with that country would need my prayers today."

Cambodia

A shiver went down my spine. Here was God doing something none of us could possibly have organised, and a wave of relief flooded my mind. With that came a renewed peace that God was going to look after our daughter.

"Now I know why the Lord gave me that thought," said Susie.

We felt we could now watch Esther go without heightened anxiety and were at last confident that God was going to take care of her while she was abroad. In the only e-mail she sent from Cambodia, she told us:

> On Sunday Jen and I ventured out to find a church. I wasn't too hopeful of success and Jen couldn't decide whether it was bravery or foolishness for us to be going out on our own. Anyway we did it and it was great. They gave us food afterwards and they got me to read some of *Love Actually* to them in English. They seemed over the moon to meet a real English person!

We even discovered that Esther became something of a celebrity in that church as people crowded round her to have a good look at her blue eyes!

In the north of Cambodia Esther visited Siem Riep, a small town where the whole group of students were expected to attend a "Meet a monk" event. It was a wet night and they sat on the floor of an upstairs room listening to a saffron-clad seventeen-year-old enlighten them about philosophy and culture. Stifled yawns could be seen as the students quickly tired of the monologue. Then, one by one, they began wandering off to sit outside in the warm evening air. In contrast Esther, never afraid to be the odd one out, "showed endless patience and humility" as she animatedly posed probing questions to this young Buddhist. In a Facebook chat later she told me, "I said 2 him. If U could summarise the teachings of the Buddha in a sentence what would that be?"

So I asked "And that was ..." And her response was, "Oh right – well it was hard to make sense of the answer, something about some teaching beginning with D? I never quite worked it out."

By this time the balmy evening had tempted all of the other students on to the veranda, and Esther was the only one who persevered until the session ended.

She was still capable of springing real surprises and used up most of her mobile phone allowance to call Ian on Father's Day. He was thrilled to hear her voice and overjoyed that she had taken the trouble to do it.

Future uncertain

Ian and Rosi

Esther wanted to remain in Glasgow over the summer. She felt that she needed time and space to formulate her plans for the future. By this time she had been referred to the university's Disability Officer. She warmed to this lady and we were pleased that she was receiving some help with her communication troubles. But the other students had moved out and she was living by herself. We were concerned that she was alone in the house most of the time. Unstable diabetes is not a condition that suits aloneness and we often felt anxious about her being by herself in the flat.

It was one of those balmy summer afternoons that should leave you without a care in the world. The sky was blue, a song thrush serenaded us from high in the eucalyptus, and the flowers blooming around us seemed to be alight with colour. We were sitting opposite each other at a slightly rickety picnic table having lunch in our garden before returning to work. But the summery scene outside contrasted sharply with the burden within.

"I can't stop thinking about her," Rosi said, as she gazed into the distance. "Any moment she could get her dose wrong, do something because she's confused and be in real trouble. There would be nobody there to see her, or help her, or even get an ambulance."

"Darling, we can't live with this. The idea that Esther could suddenly just keel over is one we can't be carrying all the time. We just can't."

We were both constantly perplexed about Esther. Anxiety was becoming our background music, the soundtrack of our thinking, and we felt helpless even though we spoke with her most days. She was definite that she wished to make her own decisions, so the most helpful thing we could do was to uphold her daily in prayer. Eventually she decided to take a voluntary suspension from her course and get a job in Glasgow. Her plan was to rejoin the following January and pick up where she'd left off. We agreed to support her in this as she felt that a rest from her studies would help her recover her stamina.

It was clear from the little Esther was saying that life was bleak for her. So determined was she to finish her course, that she couldn't come to terms with any idea of giving up. But it was obvious to the people around her that she didn't have the stamina to continue, and this tension was preying on her mind. However there were some sparks of life which lifted her spirits and ours.

"Dad, I'm going to the Isle of Skye," she announced one evening.

"That's nice, is this a holiday of some sort?"

"Nope, it's a mission trip." We were intrigued. "Some of the people from the Tron are going to do a holiday Bible club for children in a little chapel and I'm going with them."

This was just the type of venture that might lift her spirits and we detected sparks of her old enthusiasm returning. Esther had always had a passion for serving the weak and vulnerable and this venture fitted that desire well. Towards the end of her stay, however, she had been invited to her friend's wedding in the south of England and needed to get there.

"Da-a-ad." The sing-song tone of her voice told us a request was on the way. "I need to get from the Isle of Skye to Hemel Hempstead. I've been invited to a wedding. I've said yes and now I need to get there."

"That's lovely dear! Whose wedding is it?"

"Chloe's. She asked me ages ago." Chloe was a close friend and we knew she'd want to be part of the celebration.

"And when is it?"

"Saturday."

"But darling, today is Thursday! How were you thinking of getting there?"

"I thought I'd look for a bus but they don't seem to run from here."

"No, not to Hemel Hempstead. They won't run from the Isle of Skye." We tried not to laugh.

"How do I do it, then, Dad?"

"Most probably it's going to involve taking a bus, a ferry, several trains and then a taxi and it will take you all of tomorrow. Do you have anywhere to stay in Hemel?"

While she was talking we looked up the journey. It was going to take her at least seventeen hours to reach the wedding; and if anything went wrong on the journey...? We turned to prayer again. This was a major feat of organisation in which she inveigled her friends to organise the trip using cars, ferries, trains and a taxi to get to the wedding. Later on the girl who shared a caravan with Esther observed:

> She amused me with her scatterbrained-ness especially when she hadn't worked out how to get from the Isle of Skye to Hemel Hempstead for a wedding two days away.

Esther still had an endearing capacity to get people rallying round her at times like this. Somehow you just couldn't be annoyed with her!

One in the bag

Ian and Rosi

Finding occasions to meet as a family was becoming more difficult as we were all going our different ways. Nevertheless we still felt it was a priority and drove to Scotland for an August rendezvous in a guesthouse on the banks of Loch Lomond. Having developed a passion for the outdoors, Chris and Esther were very keen to climb Ben Lomond. Compared with some continental ranges, Scottish mountains might be modest in height, but walking and climbing in them can be a treacherous venture because of their latitude and exposure to weather systems. Even in summer, conditions can be atrocious; thick fog, strong winds, driving rain and freezing summit temperatures are not unusual. At over 3,000 feet, Ben Lomond is the most southerly of the Munros and Esther wanted to bag it.[1] However the weather forecast was for very poor visibility and we quickly noticed her disappointment. We only felt it would be safe to make the ascent if there was a complete change in the conditions.

It was a casual prayer. One of those "God it would be nice if ..." moments, and when we prayed that night, Rosi and I agreed nonchalantly, "Lord, it would be nice if the weather was good enough for a climb tomorrow" – and thought no more of it.

We woke up to sunshine punching through heavy cloud. Cloud still covered the summit and Esther's spirits were higher.

"Pleeeease!" She sounded like a little girl again. So after one of those family debates where every conceivable option gets an airing, we took a decision. We would start to climb along a well-marked path but as soon as there was the slightest sign of cloud around us, we would make a turn and retrace our steps. So, having kitted up and made sure we had a large-scale Ordnance map and a walkers' compass, we set off.

We started climbing, enjoying banter as we went. To our astonishment the cloud base rose ahead of us. Each time we climbed a few metres, so did the cloud it seemed, and our casual prayer of the night before was becoming a visible reality.

"Look what I can see!" shouted Esther, her voice excited by the vision before her. "The summit!" And as if with an extra spurt of energy, she strode off into the distance.

---

[1] "Munro bagging" is the sport of hill climbing each of the Scottish Munros. A walker who has climbed all 282 Munros is entitled to be called a Munroist.

Cambodia

Ian

The route we had chosen to follow had a fairly gentle incline for the majority of the distance, which eventually gave way to a scramble for the summit. By the time we had reached the final rocky portion, I was exhausted. I stopped climbing and leant against a boulder for a rest, my aching limbs refusing to be moved another inch. As I began framing thoughts of calling off the whole venture, a hand emerged from the rocks above me. Esther's head peered over the edge and I heard her call out, "Come on Dad, you can do it – you really can!"

And with that sentence memories came flooding into my mind. When Esther was facing a challenge as a child, those had been my exact words to encourage her not to give up – and now she was giving them to me. How the tables had turned! Esther's words were not a play-act or a token gesture, but an utterly genuine offer of help. My pride crumbled, my determination was renewed and my admiration for my daughter soared. In an instant her encouragement had given me the impetus to go on.

Hauling ourselves to the summit, the panoramic view was breathtaking and, in what turned out to be last picture of all five of us, we posed for someone we'd never met to take a photograph of us. That turned out to be one of those days we look back on with deep gratitude to God, and for me it enhances life enormously to know that in Him we have someone to thank.

As we look back on this single day, we see another example of God's goodness to us. Events like this created a huge bank of positive memories which we would later draw on when Esther left this world. In retrospect it taught us to take advantage of every opportunity to have positive, encouraging and just plain happy occasions together. For us, these were the things God gave us to draw strength from when times got more difficult, and the more difficult it got, the more we needed them.

The Road Not Chosen

Rosi

Although it was a memorable holiday for all the best reasons, it also had its moments of darkness. A trip around the islands of the loch was supposed to be a pleasant ride on a boat in beautiful countryside, but Esther was preoccupied. As she stood next to Ian leaning on the ship's railings, I could see she was in tears.

"Life's pants, Dad," she said. "In a week's time I have nowhere to live, and no job to go to." She added emphatically, "And I am *not* coming home, whatever."

On the one hand we could understand why she wanted to stay in Scotland to maintain her independence, but her own sense of desperation about the future was becoming more obvious. It seemed there was a deep tension in her, between an intense desire to prove her independence and an increasing awareness that she couldn't make it by herself. Given that many of her former friends were living autonomous lives by this stage, it is probable that she saw returning home not as an offer of a haven but as a retrograde step into dependence.

Our hearts were heavy over this. As parents, our reflex was to want to rescue her, to reaffirm that Baldwin Avenue could again be home if she wanted it. Nothing would have pleased us more than to express our love for her by having her in the home she'd left, and helping her in whatever she felt God was leading her to do next. But parenting is about letting go and trusting God, even when you can't see round the next corner. All we could do was to bring these burdens to God in prayer and act in faith that He could work where we had no influence.

"... And Lord," we prayed, "she needs a friend."

Cambodia

Ian

When we returned for a stopover in Glasgow, Rosi found herself in conversation with a student worker from the church who knew Esther. Her imminent need for somewhere to live was uppermost in Rosi's mind and she shared it.

"That's uncanny," he said. "I've just been handling an advert for two vacant rooms suitable for students in a house. It's an old vicarage in Anniesland. I'll tell Esther."

A few hours later I met Rosi, who was wearing a beaming smile.

"Ian," she said, "you're not going to believe this ..."

Within days, the negotiations had started and within a few weeks, Esther had moved into this rambling old house. It was to be her final move.

When she was at school in Eastbourne, one of Esther's closest friends was Christine. Although they had maintained intermittent contact, their paths had diverged since leaving school and by this time Christine had finished her first degree. She was researching for a doctorate and to Esther's delight the optimal university for her study was Glasgow. Christine too was looking for a place to live and within a month they were living in the same house, picking up the threads of friendship they had woven in the past. Esther became Christine's tour guide for all things Glaswegian and, in Christine, Esther found someone with whom she could once again be free and open. The conversational reticence that plagued Esther was forgotten in her friend's company. Later on Christine recalled:

> She could be so chatty, she used to come and sit on my bed in the evenings and tell me stories from her work or ask thoughtful questions, mainly about God or the Bible.

Not only did God provide Esther with somewhere to live and a friend to enjoy, He also provided her with a fulfilling job. Care assistant jobs are never glamorous or well paid but she relished her part-time job in a nursing home. We quickly noticed how her tone had changed in her nightly phone calls. She was animated and would talk enthusiastically about the staff and the residents, describing her duties in great (and sometimes graphic) detail.

It was only later that we discovered the significance of God's provision of this job. Some years earlier Esther had gone through a programme in our church youth group that helped the young people discover what their personal skills and gifts were. As part of this programme she had been asked to identify the group of people she felt most drawn towards. There in her workbook, at the top of the list, ringed emphatically and with scrawled arrows pointing towards the words, was her answer: "The Elderly". So here in this nursing home, an early passion was being fulfilled and she was enjoying every minute.

We hope it doesn't sound fanciful but looking back on events like these, it was almost as if God was completing His purposes in her life. He was giving her experiences which, in His wisdom, He knew would help her to thrive and find His meaning and purpose for her. Her stamina, however, was still depleted and she found working part-time as much as she could cope with.

Christmas

Ian

In contrast to her reluctance to return home in the summer, Esther seemed genuinely excited about returning to

Eastbourne for Christmas. Almost as soon as she arrived, we noticed how much more she was initiating conversation spontaneously. She was brighter and more confident, although she never spoke about her diabetes or returning to college, even though she had said it was her intention. These were closed books.

At this time she made a discovery. We had been clearing out my mother's house in advance of selling the property and acquired a pile of old CDs of hymns that Mum loved. It was while browsing through these that Esther discovered the classic song "Count your Blessings" which had struck such a deep chord with her. She played it once, then again, and once more, and it was not long before the whole house was filled with the song like a stuck record. After Esther died, we found a notebook in which she was jotting down things that had struck her during each day. She quoted Rosi:

> Esther, you have no idea how I've been blessed by your little obsession!

One of our last pictures of Esther is of her arm in arm with Rosi, dancing round the room to this song. Something had lifted and some of the carefree nature she'd enjoyed as a child was returning. We later discovered that she had started doing exactly what the song suggests and had written down the things she counted as her life's blessings. Top of this list was her friend Christine and second was her job in the nursing home.

Returning to Glasgow

Ian and Rosi

Esther returned to Glasgow and was cleared by a medic as fit to resume her course in late January. But when she restarted her studies, she did not feel the first two weeks had gone well. She seemed tired and frustrated in our nightly phone calls. One in particular brought our concerns back to the surface.

"What's happened today, Esther?"

"Went to Morrisons."

"Get anything interesting?"

"No. Just went." Her voice was monotone and staccato.

"And ...?"

"Mum, I went round their car park. I kicked over all their traffic cones. Every single one. I just ... blasted them all."

"Oh dear. What's made you so cross, darling?"

Silence.

Whether Morrisons ever noticed their traffic cones had been kicked over we will never know, but this way of venting her frustration was entirely uncharacteristic of Esther's gentle nature. In what was to be Rosi's last conversation with her, she tried to reassure Esther that she might be feeling frustrated because she was becoming a student all over again. She could no longer care for those elderly people she felt drawn to, and had to shoulder the pressure of academic work once more. Privately we were both concerned about her rising frustration and cried out to God for His help.

"Ian, I can't shake this idea that God is going to do something surprising in Esther's life, and several times I've written it down in my prayer diary."

Our nightly prayer times were now taking on a different pattern. We were asking God to help Esther cope with the stresses she was facing, and that the obvious joy she had at

Cambodia

Christmas would return to her to help her in her studies and with her friends.

And that brings us to Monday evening.

"Ian, I haven't managed to get hold of Esther for several days now."

"Neither have I. Funny, that."

"While you're out, I'll try their landline again."

"OK, See you later. Bye."

10

Mysteries

Shall we accept only good from God and not trouble? (Job 2:10)

Ian and Rosi

We will always be left with some searching questions about Esther. Was her diabetes exceptionally unstable or was she finding it too complex to handle? And if so, why? Did she manage her illness or did it manage her? It seemed to us that she was experiencing a dilemma at her deepest level. On the one hand, there was her dogged determination and her passion for independence; on the other there was a need for her to accept help from those around her. Did these come into conflict in her heart? Or had her passion for privacy about her illness become her enemy?

We shall never know the answers to these questions, and learning to live with this uncertainty is still not straightforward. However, as we look back, we are confident that God's guiding hand was on her life, particularly during the time following her diagnosis. We are still recognising that we need to leave these unanswered questions with God.

The Road Not Chosen

Sometimes it is only with hindsight that we see the broader picture of what God is doing and our part in it. So now we're going to wind the clock back and share some incidents which helped us to see God's hand at work in our story.

Discoveries

Ian

We've already told you about Esther's sharp wit and her penetrating insight into the people in her world. As an early teenager, she could be hilariously funny and reduce the room to gales of laughter by mimicking some odd characteristic in a person she'd met. These traits were so winning that we would sometimes describe Esther as "endearingly quirky". And so she was.

When she went to university, however, some of her quirks became more intense. She began covering her windows with black bin liners to keep out the light; a piece of avant-garde décor she repeated at home. But when we talked about it, even casually, she became touchy.

"If you'd like a blind, Esther," I said, "I'll put one up for you in your room. It's no problem."

But instead of her usual "Hey that would be great, Dad," she avoided my gaze, turned away and went silently into another part of the house, leaving me puzzled. She would spend many hours in her room in almost darkness, studying or just "thinking", only to emerge at mealtimes. This delightful, witty girl was slowly turning in on herself. Her intensifying introversion had become so much of an issue that the university were expressing doubts as to whether Esther would ever cope in a clinical environment. She would need to relate empathetically with patients but she was becoming more locked in her own world. She would only let those who loved her penetrate that world – and even that only happened at isolated moments.

At home, the radio was another source of tension. When it was turned on in the early morning in one part of the house, even quietly, Esther would complain from her bedroom that it was too loud. By constantly turning it down or turning it off, we would end up living in virtual silence. Banter had been replaced with reticence and we found ourselves treading on eggshells. This behaviour contrasted sharply with her attitude to songs she liked. If she got a track into her head, we'd hear it repeated over and over again at all times of the day. It was becoming unsettling to see her music listening border on the obsessional. We were worried.

We could see so clearly that something disturbing was going on, but these difficulties increasingly became no-go areas in our relationship with Esther. Her deep introversion and intense hypersensitivity to light and sound were no longer things we could avoid, but Esther was not going to let us explore them, however sensitively we broached the subjects. Our love for her was undiminished, but it was being tested by the feeling that we were increasingly locked out of areas where we would otherwise chat together naturally.

About this time Rosi went on a training course as part of her work. The needs of autistic people can easily be overlooked by social workers and health professionals, and this day was to educate them to be alert to the signs. At the end of the day we were sitting opposite each other by the kitchen table, each clutching mugs of tea. From her bag Rosi produced a sheaf of papers, singled one out and slid it across the table to me.

"Scan down that list of traits," she said, "and see who it reminds you of."

The Road Not Chosen

I started down the list, doing my best to understand each description from its printed box. I was not even half way down the page before I looked up at her.

"I know just who you're thinking of," I said, my mind beginning to go into overdrive. In that instant I couldn't bring myself to use Esther's name in relation to the title emblazoned across the top of the sheet: "Asperger's Syndrome."

"Just look!" Rosi said when I'd reached the end of the list. "Esther doesn't show any of these traits very strongly, but almost all of them are there. They're just not very intense – any of them." In the list were hypersensitivity, an intense relationship with pets, and other characteristics we had thought of as little more than her endearing quirks.

Rosi

When we returned to Glasgow for the thanksgiving service at the Tron, we felt we needed to talk to Esther's tutor. This was a planned meeting where, to our surprise, the Disability Officer (DO) who had been supporting Esther had also been invited. We thought we would approach this with some questions we wanted to explore, but we couldn't really settle on what they were. We wanted to meet these people who had been a significant part of Esther's life, but we couldn't quite identify the reasons we felt so strongly about meeting them. Perhaps it was to relive a part of her life, to fill in gaps in our knowledge, or just another twist of our personal emotional roller-coaster.

Her tutor just talked. Maybe this was her own way of processing all that had transpired. She too was trying to make sense of it all as events had moved so quickly. When she took the phone call to say Esther had died, she had been expecting the opposite.

Mysteries

"I thought you'd say Esther had come round from the coma, was sitting up in bed with a notebook and wanting to know what to do next. That would be typical!" she said.

Such was Esther's reputation for determination. Her tutor made no secret about how shocked she felt when she heard Esther had died.

"It seems unfair ... *really* unfair."

Somehow the work in the care home had released in Esther some of her potential for relating to people more confidently. This new-found assurance caused her tutor to change her assessment and pursue a clinical placement for Esther.

At this point we were taken aback by the Disability Officer. Unknown to us, Esther had been referred to the Autistic Society for help with her communication difficulties. The DO had convinced Esther this was worth doing by saying that "We are not looking for a diagnosis, it's just that you have some traits in common with people who have Asperger's Syndrome or mild autism and they may be able to help you." So from summer onwards Esther had been seeing them regularly and had pursued the goals they'd agreed with characteristic doggedness.

"She worked incredibly hard on her communication skills," said the DO, "and made exceptional progress. In fact, I want to tell you I've never seen a student as determined to succeed as Esther."

And we had noticed. At home just before she died, she'd been more voluble and had begun to take initiative once again. She'd been more relaxed and positive about the future. Esther had clearly talked to them about her Mum and Dad. They both said how positive she was about the encouragement and support she'd had from us. After all the worries and the tense moments we'd been through, this came as an enormous relief.

Her tutor could see the reality of Esther's faith and how profound it was.

"She was a very deep girl," she said. "When other students were trivial, Esther was deep and this marked her out as different. She was almost other-worldly. In this world, but not of it!"

We discussed her continuing on the course and they both commented that Esther had not indicated that she was considering any other option but to complete it. This was reassuring because we had wondered whether or not we should have raised this with her. It also shed some light on an unanswered question for us. One of Esther's last entries on her Facebook page was "Esther has a big decision to make", but she concealed what this decision was. Knowing some of her personal struggles, we think this may have been the decision of whether to complete her course.

Unanswered questions

Ian

Knowing this, we felt an intense need to discover more about the circumstances that led to Esther's death, although we knew some of our questions would probably never be resolved. We felt that more information than we had at the time would help us understand what happened and forge a way of coping in the future. But we knew it was risky. Suppose we unearthed something about her life we would rather not have discovered?

Esther had been diagnosed with diabetes when she was twenty-one in 2007. Despite spending four nights in hospital and still learning how to do the four daily injections of insulin, she had been doggedly determined to return to Scotland to continue her course. She had been referred to the diabetic clinic in Glasgow, and because her diabetes was unstable she had been for frequent appointments. But these appointments did not always go to plan.

"Dad, I worked really hard at recording my eating, exercising and blood sugars but the nurse just took no notice." Her crestfallen voice betrayed frustration that her efforts were not being recognised.

We had a long list of unanswered questions about the nature of her treatment and the effectiveness of the support she had received. Glitches in communication between the different professionals involved in her care was a common theme. What had really caused her to slip into a diabetic coma only two weeks after a consultant had considered her fit enough to return to her course?

We composed a long and detailed letter to the consultant who had treated her. We just spilled it all out. Signs of depression, unusual behaviour and Esther's feelings about not being heard by the professionals: they all got an airing. We expected a brief, matter-of-fact response but we received an even more lengthy reply recording the hospital's view on each of the issues we'd raised. Not everything we read satisfied us and we could have analysed and debated but were not sure where that would get us.

We were grateful that an otherwise busy consultant had taken time to address our questions seriously. But we were faced with a choice: to challenge points we disagreed with, or to accept that little would be gained on either side by a fight. So we took a conscious decision to leave it there. We took reassurance in the fact that the staff had clearly given Esther time and advice and had done their best for her, but there remained some mystery about why her diabetes had appeared so difficult to manage. Deciding to accept the consultant's response went some way to preventing a sense of blame and bitterness from taking root. We were beginning to realise we might never know the answers, and God's best was for us to learn to live with the questions.

11

Hope

Learn from yesterday, live for today and hope for tomorrow. The important thing is not to stop questioning. (Albert Einstein)

We know that suffering produces perseverance, perseverance produces character and character produces hope. And hope doesn't disappoint because God has poured his love into our hearts. (Romans 5:3-5 paraphrase)

Ian

Now a change of gear. So far in our book we have been unfolding our story and adding reflections as we go. It's now time for us to switch direction and pull together some of the threads that have been left in the air. There are several motives behind this. You may just be interested in the story, or you may be walking this path of loss yourself. Alternatively you may be alongside a friend or family member who is currently grieving the loss of someone they love, and God has placed you in their lives to be a comfort and support to them. Whatever your position in relation to our story, we'd like to take a moment to stand back from the events, and set down some of the things that we have learned from the experiences you've just read about.

As a reader you may or may not share our Christian faith but I hope you can see that it would be hard for us to make sense of our journey without it. Of course you're allowed to be a little cynical and say, "Well he's a minister, he would say this sort of thing, wouldn't he?" and I have some sympathy with that feeling. I would like to think, however, that I'd react and apply my faith in the same way regardless of being a church leader or involved in Christianity professionally. That can only ever be conjecture on my part but I hope you've detected that being a Christian goes far beyond merely accepting a set of beliefs or adopting certain religious practices. There is a deeply relational side to Christianity that leaves me uncomfortable about even using the word "religion" to describe it. When five-year-old Esther asked me how far we had to go on our holiday journey, I'm sure she had a child's awareness that something worth having lay at the end of it. We've discovered that with Christ at our side it is possible to end up better people at the end of our grieving journey, however painful it may be along the way.

God's comfort

The comfort we receive from God is real comfort. It isn't unfeeling stoicism that blandly says, "Oh, God knows best", grits its teeth and carries on regardless. It is a profound sense of His love and acceptance which develops as we get to know Him better.

When, as a little girl, Esther fell over and grazed her knees, she would come running to me with tears streaming down her face for a cuddle. She would not analyse whether her father cared or what evidence could be adduced to support her assertion, she just fell into my arms. While our parenting can only ever be a pale reflection of God's Fatherhood, we need to be like her when we turn to Him for comfort. We need to fall into His arms and accept without reserve the love and comfort He offers us. This is not a sign of weakness, it is a sign that we know who we really are, that we belong to Him and are accepted by Him unconditionally.

The Bible is peppered with passages which feed our souls with God's comfort and produce strength for times like these. King David said:

> I sought the Lord and he answered me and delivered me from all my fears ... taste and see that the Lord is good! Blessed (happy, to be envied) is the one who takes refuge in him. (Psalm 34:4-8)

In a letter to the church in Ephesus, St Paul prayed that his readers would be

> ... strengthened in your inner being and know, intimately, the love of God which surpasses human knowledge. (Ephesians 3:16-19 paraphrase).

So how does being a Christian affect the way we grieve? First of all, let's acknowledge that it doesn't take away the pain. Loss hurts whether you regard yourself as a Christian or not. But knowing that we're loved by God and He has our best interests at heart changes the way we go about grieving. For Rosi and me, being grievers is not merely a problem to be solved or a circumstance we must somehow get through; it's a calling God places on our lives to assist us to become the rounded people He desires us to be: secure in ourselves and secure in Him. When St Paul was writing about one particularly painful situation in his own life (and he never identified exactly what it was) he described it as a "thorn" that had been given to him by God. But far from it being purposeless pain, Paul saw it as a way of proving to himself (and therefore to us) that God's grace is "sufficient", even when we feel weak. He put it like this:

> In order to keep me from becoming conceited, I was given a thorn in my flesh, ... Three times I pleaded with the Lord to take it away from me. But he said to me, "My grace is sufficient for you, for my power is made perfect in weakness." (2 Corinthians 12:9 paraphrase)

So the supply of God's grace is what we really need if we are to be resilient, especially when we taste the acid of grief. Sometimes, when life was at its most difficult, we found that receiving His grace needed to be done through a conscious choice rather than relying on it happening naturally. When we are so weak as to have no personal resources left, any spiritual or emotional power we experience has to come from Him. But there is a danger here. It would be easy to become haughty about being the recipient of such a supply of personal strength from outside ourselves. We cannot take any credit for it. So Paul prefaces his description of the thorn with a phrase that is often overlooked. God's purpose, in part at least, for the thorn in Paul's life was to "keep [him] from becoming conceited."

Grieving has that effect. It has an uncanny knack of wearing down our hubris and diluting our pride. A man who is at his wits' end and weeping buckets because of his loss (as I was at times) can no longer pretend to be a hero among his family and friends. Any conceit evaporates as the people closest to him see the broken man he has become. It is in moments like these that relying on God's power becomes the only way to live – even the only way to survive. Pride is of no value. Grief is a great leveller.

But when we are in this powerless state, there is another dynamic that can come into play. Those whom I allowed to be closest to me at my lowest were the very people through whom I felt God's love. "My grace", which Paul heard God speak about, is not an ethereal quality that can be fully understood only by theologians and the deeply religious. It is a source of down-to-earth daily strength that I found mediated through my family's fellowship, support and love. It's an expression of God's generosity and it lifted me from my pain, often almost imperceptibly, by the drip feed of comfort and love they gave to me, especially Rosi, Christopher and Polly. I hope I was able to give it to them too.

In his earlier life St Paul was trained as a Hebrew scholar who mixed with the highest echelons of Jewish society. So when he used the word "perfect" he brought to it a Hebraic, not an English, understanding of perfection. For English speakers the concept of perfection is dominated by the idea of flawlessness – a perfect diamond or a perfect performance for example. But for Paul it also carried the concept of completion. Some translations of the Bible carry this wording. God's grace being "made perfect" means that the full picture of His grace is only comprehended when we receive it in times of pain. Knowing God's generosity in times of joy, satisfaction, peace, achievement or just in run-of-the-mill living is wonderful, but it is only part of the story. Our perception of His grace is incomplete, says Paul, until we receive it in our trials. There is something lacking in our experience of God until we find Him in our suffering and pain.

Secondly, knowing we are loved by God helps us to see our grieving from a higher perspective. I hope that doesn't sound pretentious because it isn't intended to be. There are many events in life that we can't explain and it would be easy to cynically ask, "How could a God of love allow Esther's death to happen?" I certainly asked that in my darker moments. But that question assumes that love never sees beyond our present personal immediate well-being. It ignores the existence of any bigger picture.

The Road Not Chosen

In my childhood, there were times when my father, Will White, left me mystified. Why, for example, did he insist on holding my hand as we walked down our busy high street? I remember tugging at him to be free to run, but the more I tugged, the tighter his grip became. When I was older and had more freedom, he would advise me not to cycle into certain parts of the town, and to avoid hanging around with the gang of lads that gravitated to the end of our street. What a spoil-sport! Or so I thought.

There was, however, another reality to our relationship. These restrictions were the exceptions, not the rule. The vast bulk of evidence told me that Dad loved my brother and me, cared for us profoundly, and was passionately committed to the welfare of our family. The comfort I received from him when I was in any kind of trouble was real and deeply felt. When I became a teenager I could of course have adopted a more sceptical approach and mistrusted my father's motives, but that would deny the weight of evidence around me. My Dad loved me still and I knew it! A cynical attitude would also have put me in a place where I assumed my knowledge was superior to his. A similar dynamic applies in our relationship with God. Although we don't understand (and don't like!) some of the experiences He brings across our path, we know He is deeply and passionately committed to the welfare of His children. In Him we have a confidence that His desire for us is for our good and His credit and, for me, that makes Him all the more trustworthy.

In a classic book about why it's reasonable to believe in a God of love, the Manhattan church leader Tim Keller says this:

> We see lurking within supposedly hard-nosed scepticism an enormous faith in one's own cognitive faculties. If our minds can't plumb the depths of the

universe for good answers to suffering, well, then, there can't be any! This is blind faith of a high order.[1]

Throughout our time of grieving (and after six years it still continues), Rosi and I have tried to keep our focus on the really big evidences of God's love and care for us. There are many things we don't understand about God and why He cares so passionately for us, but losing Esther has made me a more grateful person. No day is ever a piece of fluff that can be frittered away.

So we have tried not to let the things we can't understand interfere with the realities we experience. It requires some emotional heavy lifting (and a touch of humility) but it allows God to be who He says He is – a God of love, comfort, compassion and justice.

Being a comforter

When Esther died I had to drink my own medicine. As a minister, I often help bereaved families navigate public funerals and private grieving, but this was entirely different. With Esther's death, Rosi and I were on the receiving end of other people's care. For the most part that was a healing and uplifting experience, but not always. So what made the difference? Grieving is such a universal experience that most of us, at some point in our lives, encounter people who are experiencing a deep loss. At the same time it's a very individual experience because each of us grieves in a subtly different way. So are there ways we can act or react that will help bring reassurance and comfort? We feel there are; so here, with some trepidation, is our etiquette for comforters. It's based on the experiences you've already read about and we hope it will be useful to you when someone grieving crosses your path.

---

[1] Tim Keller, *The Reason for God,* Hodder and Stoughton: London, 2008

The Road Not Chosen

Please don't avoid the bereaved

Just because words may be difficult to find, this should never be a reason for giving a grieving person a wide berth. They need your caring interest more now than at any other time and a few words of encouragement will always be helpful, even if you think they sound bland. C S Lewis observed how isolated loss made him feel:

> An odd by-product of my loss is that I'm aware of being an embarrassment to everyone I meet. At work, at the club, in the street, I see people, as they approach me, trying to make up their minds whether they'll "say something about it" or not ... Some funk it altogether.[1]

To have the experience of walking through the church or the town and someone grasp my arm for just a second and say "We're thinking of you" before moving on was enormously supportive. It reassured me that *that* person at *that* moment had noticed us, looked into our eyes and not remained silent. We'd been acknowledged.

Please be swift to listen and slow to speak

One of the most precious things our friends gave us during this period was their time. Although in the early days the constant repetition of the events became harrowing, it was wonderful to be listened to. You may recall how we discovered we could lessen the anguish by using the same collection of sentences to describe events. Unforced, uncritical listening is highly therapeutic and at times we bathed in the warmth of it. However, if you say to a grieving friend "How are you today?" do be prepared for any answer – including a non-answer. Sometimes we just didn't want to respond to the question and

---

[1] C S Lewis, *A Grief Observed*, Faber and Faber: London, 1961

skirted round it to talk about something else. The wise comforters just ignored this and swam with our red herring. There were a few occasions when people just wouldn't give up and virtually insisted on a progress report on our grieving, even when we found it difficult to verbalise. They probably wanted to be reassured we were "getting better", even at times when we were struggling.

Please avoid offering answers

The most helpful people were the ones who didn't try to give us answers ("Oh if I was you I'd do this ...") or make comparisons ("I always do that ... why don't you?"), but did nothing more than keep an open mind without jumping to conclusions about us or our well-being. They listened without judging, heard without criticising and paid attention without showing alarm. The most reassuring people didn't use words like "ought" or "should", they just accepted us at face value, even in moments when the face wasn't pretty. It is this uncritical listening that was so helpful to us and has taught me not to feel that something must always be spoken when trying to help a grieving friend.

Please accept feelings at face value

We expect grieving people to feel sad but there is a wide variety of other emotions that can take us by surprise. For example, bereaved people can feel anger. I did. That anger may be directed at medics (they didn't do what I expected them to), at family (why didn't my relatives notice what was happening?) and particularly at God (if He's sovereign, why did He let this happen?) The last one is especially troubling for Christians because we want to experience God as our loving heavenly Father and yet paradoxically rage at Him for allowing a death to take place. In reality it's OK to be angry with God. He is big enough to handle it. But on at least one occasion when I revealed my own feelings of fury, I was told by someone in no uncertain terms that, "As a minister, you shouldn't feel like that." I did not feel comforted! Other people are allowed to feel loneliness, guilt, self-reproach, anxiety, fear, numbness, shock or relief but as a minister I am not. Or so it seemed. Being a minister makes no difference to my status as a human being and the Bible teaches that we are equally loved by God regardless of the work we're called to do. It was the people who just took Rosi and me at face value, whatever our emotional state, who were the ones who brought the deepest reassurance.

Rosi and I did feel some sense of relief although we were uneasy about it. I hope you have gleaned from our story how difficult life was likely to have been for Esther had she survived, especially if she had been brain-damaged. For some time we struggled with whether we were being callous to think this way. But with the benefit of hindsight, we are genuinely relieved she has been spared that agony.

Please pay attention to the messages that aren't spoken

The words we hear from people who grieve are only ever the tip of their personal iceberg. I play keyboards in a band and when we perform, there will be a bass guitar playing for most of the gig. The bass rarely plays a solo but always provides the deep musical foundation above which the other instruments and vocals are heard more prominently. Our conversations are often like that band. The words are the sounds that are heard most prominently but the bass line is the foundation of feelings that can be concealed beneath the spoken word.

Therefore, identifying the emotional bass line is vital if we are genuinely to empathise. We glean a great deal of information about each other without saying a word. Even over the telephone, we can learn about a person's state from the tone and cadence of their voice. Then, when we are face to face, we can detect enthusiasm, boredom, or irritation from expressions which flash across the face, sometimes for only a fraction of a second. Noticing the set of the mouth, the slope of the shoulders and the way someone is standing or sitting provides clues we shouldn't ignore. So listening to the non-verbal emotional bass line of someone who is grieving will help you to be a genuine help to them.

There were times when someone would come to me and say "Seems like you're not doing too well today? ..." and show by their own body language they had noticed where I was struggling with life. This simple act was enormously reassuring because they had spotted my non-verbal message and responded empathetically to it.

Tiers of loss

Not every loss is the same. When we think of loss we can mistakenly assume that it only affects our past. But losses are not that simple and we find they affect our present and future with different intensities. In my pastoral practice, I think of losses as coming in several tiers which vary according to their severity and which we handle in different ways. As we have lost Esther and come to terms with her death, we have found different losses cropping up in our lives that all revolve around missing our daughter.

The more severe the loss, the deeper the reaction we have to it and the longer it takes to find recovery. Rosi and I have found that understanding this process helps us with everything from handling minor frustrations to the traumas we've been describing in this book. We then realised that if we learn how to handle the minor losses of life, we will have a spiritual and emotional toolkit ready for when the major traumas arrive.

The Road Not Chosen

Casual

Casual losses are the misadventures we experience most weeks of the year. Yesterday, for example, I went into my favourite coffee shop to buy a drink. In this shop I can claim a discount if I take one of their cups with me, but as I walked through the door I realised I had left this special cup in my car. My loss? A mere twenty-five pence but I still chided myself for being forgetful. In that fleeting moment my reaction was nothing more than a shrug and I recovered from the loss in a matter of minutes (helped by a dose of caffeine, no doubt). But suppose a friend had noticed this, put his arm round my shoulder and adopted an earnest voice to say "Ian, I'm *so* sorry you didn't get your 25p discount," I would be a little mystified and think that he was exaggerating the impact of my loss. Recovery from casual losses is straightforward and most of us do it without effort.

Minor

Minor losses are events we choose not to ignore like my casual loss of the missed discount. While writing this chapter, I have taken some annual leave to complete the job. But an unexpected development in the church meant I had to attend a meeting, make some phone calls and send some e-mails. This put my writing schedule back so I may now miss my own deadline, and Rosi may see a bit less of me when she comes in from work today. Of course I adopted a contented, cheerful attitude for the meeting (as a leader, that is the right thing to do), but privately I felt miffed.

The effect of minor losses of this order is usually minor frustration. They are often the result of a blocked goal (I wanted to finish by the end of the day) which has knock-on effects (I won't finish when I'd hoped to). But they are still minor in comparison to losing one's daughter. My reaction to the minor loss was mild annoyance which I continued to feel for the rest of the day. I had to reschedule my diary. But recovery from these setbacks is usually accomplished within the rhythm of a day, and after a good night's sleep I'd almost forgotten about it.

Significant

As their name suggests, significant losses have a deeper impact on my life and therefore take more time for recovery. They are felt when prospects I would otherwise reasonably expect to enjoy are taken away. The more important the prospect is to my sense of who I am, the more intensely I feel it.

The important factor identifying significant losses is that the thing or the prospect I've lost may never be recoverable. This permanence of loss causes me to look at it in a different way. If, for example, my health means I can no longer drive a car, my mobility is impaired for ever. If I am passed over for promotion in my workplace, I may never have that job I really worked for because someone else is now doing it.

Significant losses have a perpetual quality to them which means that I won't usually recover by having the thing I've lost restored to me again. It is *I* who have to change if I'm going to face life with energy and vitality once more. Some reworking of who I am needs to be done, and it may take weeks or longer before I feel back to normal.

Just as important is the effect these losses have on my self-image. They are the kinds of events which cause me to ask questions about myself and my capacity to do the things I previously took for granted. So I may now need the help of sympathetic friends all the more, both to listen to me sensitively and to help me readjust my perspectives.

The Road Not Chosen

Intense

Losses are often made more intense if they involve deeply personal relationships. Losing my father was an intense loss. As a church leader and mentor he had been an example to me for the whole of my life, so to anticipate life without him, even on the end of the phone, caused me great angst. Major financial losses such as losing a job or retirement can also come into this category. My reaction to an intense loss may not be as controllable compared with lesser losses. I may find myself weeping in private moments and having intense longings for life to be back where it was before the loss. At a previous church we helped a talented young woman through the trauma of a broken engagement, and the sense of loss, both for herself and her prospects, was intense. Another friend has been diagnosed with Altzheimer's and he spoke very movingly with us about his memory lapses and his descent into a world of his own which no longer connects with others as it used to. He told us about how he would weep with his wife at home, especially when thinking of what to say next was impossible. The intensity of his loss was plain to all of us in the room.

Jesus Christ's experience of losing his close friend Lazarus comes into this category (John11:1-44). It gave rise to the shortest verse in the Bible that bluntly states "Jesus wept." Even though the account in John's gospel hints that Jesus knew something remarkable was about to happen (Lazarus was to be raised to life), it still hit Jesus very hard.

It may take months even to begin to come to terms with the effects of intense losses like these, and Rosi and I often observe that the people who come through them best are those who already have a good network of friends to support them. Our friends were vital and we couldn't have recovered to the extent we have today without their help and compassion. Too often we overlook how vital human relationships are, in our attempts to medicalise or analyse human behaviour. Intense losses need deep relationships to assist in rebuilding life.

Crucial

Crucial losses are the most acute that life can throw at us. They are the most painful experiences we feel and can take the longest time in recovery – in the order of years. In a classic 1967 study two psychiatrists, Thomas Holmes and Richard Rahe[1], examined the medical records of over five thousand patients to determine whether or not stressful events cause illnesses. They gave each of these patients a list of 43 stressful events and asked them to attach a measure of intensity to each event. Their results showed what had long been suspected, that there is a measurable link between stress and illness. They also demonstrated that increased amounts of stress diminish our capacity to recover. Their table (the Social Readjustment Rating Scale) ranked these events from the most stressful to the least. Today we take it for granted that stressful events can upset our health. But significantly the top six items of their table, those which cause the most stress in adults, are all losses[2] and each of them comes into our "crucial" category.

When I experience a crucial loss my whole being is consumed by the thought of it. In the early stages, it dominates my thinking day and night so that everything in life is interpreted through its lens. Many grieving people, and we were no different, find this crucial loss creates a lack of focus and unpredictable weeping that is not easy to control, even in public. For me it knocked my concentration for six (as you have already discovered) and neither of us was able to work effectively. I suspect Jesus' experience in the garden of

---

[1] Holmes TH, Rahe RH, "The Social Readjustment Rating Scale", *Journal Psychosom Res,* 1967, Vol 11, No 2, pp 213–8.

[2] Death of a spouse, divorce, marital separation, imprisonment, death of a close family member and personal injury or illness.

Gethsemane shortly before His death comes into this category (Luke 22:39-46).

With crucial losses we think less in terms of recovery and more in terms of living a different life. It may take years to return to normality and it will be a different kind of normality. Then the assurance of the Bible is that, with God's help, we can end up stronger people at the end than we were at the beginning.

So?

And now for the reason we're delving into this. When Esther died we knew we had "lost" our daughter. She will never be with us on this earth again and we have had to rework our approach to life as a consequence. But losing the person was not the only loss surrounding Esther's death. We lost the prospects of seeing her develop as a woman, seeing her work at a career, experiencing her love and interest in us as parents as well as touching details like the cheery way she always said "Hello!" as she came through the front door. We lost the joy of giving to her and of her giving to us. So Esther's death brings multifaceted losses that come into all the categories we've described.

Looking back on the time since Esther died, we have come to realise how important it is to be prepared for losses. We never know when they will arrive or how intense they will be. But we have both found that the experience of going through lesser losses equips us for the greater ones. Even talking together about how we are handling tough events in life helps us to crystallise how God is at work and how we can best follow Him.

Losing Esther has also had one consequence I didn't expect. I find myself wanting to make the most of every single day. We never know which day will be our last, and we have both learned that living without regrets and taking every opportunity for spiritual development that comes our way is the only way to live.

We've also learned to invest in relationships. Losing Esther has reawakened friendships with people with whom we had almost lost touch. In the busyness of work, we relegated some of these friendships to second place behind growing a thriving church. But relegating people is always a miscalculation, and we are seeking to rectify it because when we lost Esther it was people, not projects, that fed us with God's love. It was our friends, real friends, who were the vehicles of His comfort, even though some of them didn't realise it at the time.

The symphony of grieving

I am a lover of classical music and will pay serious money to listen to a symphony being performed. Throughout my life I have marvelled at the capacity of orchestral composers to take a simple sequence of notes and turn them into a symphonic work which keeps me listening intently, sometimes for over an hour. In every symphony there are musical themes which are introduced, developed and repeated throughout the piece. They are the building blocks of the music and without them the work loses its structure and meaning. A theme may be played by the entire string section with all the brass on top. It's loud, it's bold, it's strident, and we can't possibly miss it. On other occasions, the same theme will not be quite so obvious. It may be played by a quieter part of the orchestra or modified so we're not fully aware of its presence. Occasionally a theme may be so subtly mutated that we might not recognise it at all until we look at the music in retrospect.

I want to suggest that our grieving is similar to a symphony in which common themes recur. Sometimes we will encounter them at top volume where they can't be avoided. It may feel as if it is the only thing we're experiencing at that moment. At other times they may appear less obviously while other things are going on in life. Then occasionally one of the themes may appear so subtly that we hardly recognise it until we reflect on life retrospectively.

In 1917 Sigmund Freud published one of the first careful studies on grieving and was the first person to use the phrase "grief work" to describe the emotional heavy lifting we carry out when recovering from a crucial loss.[1] But it was in 1969 that Elizabeth Kubler-Ross, inspired by her work with terminally ill patients, wrote her book *On Death and Dying*.[2] She described the five "stages of grief" she observed in her practice, as people came to terms with both their own mortality and the loss of a loved one. This book gave way to an extensive new literature on the process of grieving. Since then we have come to recognise that grieving is less of a sequence of steps and more akin to a collection of recurring themes.

While we tend not to experience these themes in a predefined order, there are some patterns. The first two tend to occur in our early time of grieving and the last two later on. But any of them can occur with different intensities at almost any moment, so being aware of them can help us to cope with our losses. They are neither linear nor universal. However, as we look back, Rosi and I have seen these working out in our own narrative and you will, we hope, have observed them as we have told our story.

---

[1]   Freud S., "Mourning and Melancholia", from *The Collected Papers of Sigmund Freud, Vol 4*, Trans J Riviere: (Hogarth Press: London, 1925). (The papers were published originally in 1917 and first appeared in English in 1925)

[2]   Kubler-Ross E., *On Death and Dying*: (Scribner Classics: New York, 1969)

Hope

The Isolation Theme

Often our first reaction to hearing about the serious illness or death of a loved one is to avoid truly believing it. We try to rationalise what would otherwise be overwhelming news by continuing to operate normally, as if we are denying its reality. We put the news in the mental box of "just another thing to cope with today", and this denial is a normal reaction to traumatic news. We find we need to defend ourselves at the emotional level, isolating ourselves from the events. We feel we are observing someone else's life and that the events are not really happening to us. By restricting ourselves to the cognitive world we buffer the immediate impact of the news, and it is this temporary response that carries us through the first wave of pain. I now find it hard to believe that with Esther seriously ill in hospital, we could sit in the back of Kit's car organising our office work as if it was just another day.

The Rage Theme

As the masking effect of our intense disbelief subsides, so the strong emotions that have been developing beneath the surface need to find an outlet. Often that outlet shows itself in frustration and anger. The anger may be aimed at inanimate objects, people in authority (like the Glasgow undertaker), complete strangers (like the revellers on the road into Glasgow), or even family members who are close to us.

Anger is often the consequence of a blocked goal when something to which we had pinned our hopes is taken away. The joy we had hoped to experience and the love we'd expected to give Esther had all been removed by events beyond our control. So hope, the hope of all that Esther meant in the present and might mean to us in the future, had been dashed. There were times when we felt angry: angry enough to raise our voices and vent our frustration.

Martha and Mary's frustration at Jesus' delaying His visit to Lazarus is an example of this (John 11:17-20). The Bible doesn't record explicitly the tone of voice Martha used when she met Jesus, but the text sounds as if she was being sharp with Him. They were helpless and vulnerable and their goal of seeing Jesus heal Lazarus had been blocked.

The Bargaining Theme

A normal reaction to feelings of helplessness and vulnerability is a need to regain control by bargaining. We will want to *do* something or *give* something in the hope that we will *gain* something in return. "If only we had sought medical attention sooner" or "If only we had tried to be better parents" are bargaining positions we take up. Secretly, we may make deals with God in an attempt to postpone the inevitable or change the past. This bargaining theme is often marked by asking the "If only" questions, and we see it in the story of Martha and Mary. "Lord," Martha said to Jesus, "if only you had been here my brother would not have died." (John 11:21)

We can become lost in a jumble of "If only..." or "What if..." hypotheses, as if we could go back in time to change our history. Guilt is often bargaining's companion. The "If only" statements have us finding fault with ourselves and inventing what we could have done differently, while knowing all along that nothing can change the past.

The Depressive Theme

That dawning realisation that the past can never be changed is one factor giving rise to the depressive theme. This theme tends to show itself in two guises. The first is a reaction to practical implications relating to the loss. Sadness and regret predominate in this type of depression and we may worry about the cost of the funeral and coping with the arrangements which go alongside it.

The second type of depression is more subtle and more pervasive. It is our internal preparation to separate from our loved one and say our final goodbyes. We feel emptiness and grief enter our lives on a deeper level than we ever imagined. This depressive theme feels as though it will never end, so life may appear hopeless. It is a dark place to be and we now understand that this is an appropriate response to a great loss. Deep sadness (or *anhedonia* – a lack of joy) is too often seen as unnatural and needing to be fixed, especially among Christians. But we can't easily snap out of joylessness and, while we may sometimes need professional help, this is a normal reaction to the intensity of great loss. It is part of the way God made us and is one of the many steps along the road towards healing; a road that He walks with us.

There is evidence of this in Psalm 22. David thought he had completely lost touch with God and was grieving the absence of intimate communion with Him. He expressed it in graphic language:

> I am poured out like water and all my bones are out of joint. My heart has turned to wax, it has melted away within me. My strength is dried up like a potsherd and my tongue sticks to the roof of my mouth. You lay me in the dust of death. (Psalm 22:14-15)

In common with many of us, he saw physical symptoms emerging which were manifestations of his deep emotional turmoil. His language showed the intensity of his *anhedonia*. But the fact that David was still speaking to God (even if God didn't appear to respond) indicated he still believed there was an ear that could hear him.

The Road Not Chosen

The Turning Theme

As life begins to return to normal, our emotions can make an upward turn and we gradually begin to feel anticipation about the future. Gradually the things that we once enjoyed, before the bereavement, begin to hold attraction for us again. The difference between the depressive theme and the turning theme is the presence of hope. In Psalm 22 there is a moment when David begins writing in the future tense:

> I will declare your name to my brothers; in the congregation I will praise you. (Psalm 22:22)

At that point he was not yet praising God, but he was anticipating the day when praise would again be on his lips. With this he began to acknowledge that God had been listening to him all along his journey, even though David had not been aware of it:

> For [God] has not despised or disdained the suffering of the afflicted one. He has not hidden his face from him but listened to his cry for help. (Psalm 22:24)

The Acceptance Theme

It is this theme that gives us confidence to face the future without pain. It is said that Queen Elizabeth, the Queen Mother, was once asked if she had got over the loss of her husband, King George VI. She is supposed to have replied, "One doesn't get over it, but one does get used to it." This aphorism sums up the acceptance theme. It is identified by the feeling that most of the grief work has been completed, even though there may still be some unfinished business. A dawning sense of calm shows we have traversed some of the choppier water of our grieving and can look forward with renewed confidence. As we begin hearing this theme, we feel free to make plans for the future and look at life through a more positive lens.

At one of my lowest points I remember wrestling with God while walking up a steep hill in Eastbourne. Tears were streaming down my face as I cried out to Him, "For pity's sake will You get us to a place where we don't look at Esther's life with all this pain! I just can't take much more!" It was a prayer from the heart that occasionally I still echo, but much less often than I did at that time.

So for now we look back on her death with hurt but not torment, with aches but not agony, and we feel this change is part of God's goodness to us. But we recognise we are the lucky ones as this gift is not afforded to everyone. Grieving is as individual as loving, and there is no right or wrong way to come to terms with deep loss. We are each individuals who will respond differently to mourning as we encounter its twists and turns. Our hope is that reading this story will help you towards hearing your own acceptance theme, as the writing of it has helped us.

Living with mystery

Will "closure" ever arrive? We often wonder whether it's realistic to expect to come to a place where the loss of Esther is a process completed. Looking back over the journey we've travelled so far, we doubt if that will ever happen. And our main reasons for thinking this way are the consequences of it happening. Suppose we came to a point where Esther's life was just a thing that happened to us, like a holiday or a visit to the dentist. Surely that would devalue the life we were given for such a short span of time.

The Road Not Chosen

When I take a funeral I often use these words when I lead the family in prayer:

> ... and Lord, should there be any feelings of regret that we failed to do something – grant us your forgiveness. Grant healing where there is hurt. Grant trust where there is doubt. Grant hope where there is sadness.

And of all the words used in funerals, I find these to be some of the most powerful. They are medicine we have now taken for ourselves. They bring release and hope to all of us who wrestle with the loss of someone we love.

We've also learned about being gentler with ourselves. This experience has taught us that we cannot ride victoriously through every situation we face and remain untouched by it. The way we handle loss moulds us into different people from the ones we were before it happened. We've found ourselves working towards being better rather than bitter, facing pain instead of shrinking from it. We hope this has made us deeper people, more able to empathise with others who grieve, whatever their loss may be.

We've also learned to trust God in a new way – the way of faith that doesn't have a full understanding of His plan. We like to think we can solve any problem or overcome any hurdle. But in the end that's nothing more than hubris. Far better to live in such a way as to maximise gratitude and minimise regret. And we have only been able to do this by resting our confidence more in God's promises and less in our own feelings.

We still carry a niggling anxiety that we might forget Esther. We fear that the memory of her cheerful voice, her quirky humour and her chaotic living space will fade so far into the distance that she will no longer be part of us. But facing these fears helps us to live more in touch with God and with ourselves. We are discovering how liberating it is to live each

Hope

day without unfinished business because endings can arrive so unexpectedly.

Esther's death will remain a mystery, but as we have walked (and continue to walk) the road not chosen, we agree with Paul that because of God's love, "We do not grieve as those who have no hope." We genuinely don't, although it was a close-run thing at times.

Postscript

Ian

Throughout this book it has been Rosi and I who have been telling the events in our story. But Esther's death affected Chris and Polly every bit as much as it did us. Their story is different from ours and they have courageously walked their own journey of grieving.

The expedition Chris, Polly and Esther were planning, to walk the West Highland Way, did eventually take place. Chris and Polly braved the remnants of a tropical hurricane to walk all 107 miles in seven days. They did it to honour Esther and to raise money for the Esther White Fund which was also used to help them fund a later mission trip.

However, while they were wrestling with the loss of Esther, they were also facing a major challenge of their own. Here is how they described it on their web page:

> We found out in 2009 that we had a very low chance of having our own children. After a few more investigations we found out that the probability was less than 3% without complex IVF treatment and there were no other options. We felt certain that IVF was not God's plan for us so we declined the intervention and began to investigate adopting a child.
>
> In June 2013 Polly was feeling a bit under the weather and after a week without a clear diagnosis she did a test just to eliminate pregnancy from the causes and discovered she was seven weeks pregnant!

The Road Not Chosen

On the morning of the birth Rosi and I could barely contain our excitement. The phone rang and I heard Chris's excited voice on the line above the sound of a crying baby.

"Can you hear that, Dad?"

"You bet! What a wonderful sound! Are you both OK?"

"We're fine. Polly's shattered but happy – and you've got a granddaughter!" At that point he paused and his voice became more earnest. "Dad, would you mind if we used Esther's name as one of hers, or would that feel ... weird?"

"Chris, nothing would thrill us more than to know Esther's name lives on, but it's entirely your call."

"In that case she'll be called April Esther," he said. Then as soon as the line went dead, we began packing our bags to visit them. Chris continued on his web page:

> At 7.50 a.m. on the first of March 2014 April Esther White was born weighing 9lb 9oz. We are so thrilled that she is in the world with us and can't wait to start life as a family of three. We have always known this was within God's power, but are still overwhelmed that He has actually involved us in His miracle.
>
> Do not be anxious about anything, but in everything, by prayer and petition, with thanksgiving, present your requests to God (Philippians 4:6).

Before you leave

You might like to share your thoughts about *The Road Not Chosen* on this web page, where you can also discover the reactions of other readers:

www.facebook.com/TheRoadNotChosen

To find out about the Esther White Fund you can browse to:

www.whites.me.uk/EstherWhiteFund

Heaven Day

Weeping may endure for a night, but joy comes in the morning
(Psalm 30:5)

When our friends in Grand Cayman invited us to stay with them, we knew we would pray a momentous prayer there. Although it will never touch your soul in the same way it touched ours, we hope you will meet with God as you read it and catch a glimpse of the person we loved for twenty-two years.

Dear Lord, today would have been Esther's birthday but we're renaming it her Heaven Day. There was something unique about Esther from the day she came to us. To have our daughter born on the same day of the year that Ian was born again made her so precious to us from the moment she entered this world.

We thank You for her unusual character qualities of gentleness and kindness which so many of her friends valued. When leaving junior school she was given a mug that was full of slips of paper on which her classmates had written comments about her. It moved us to discover almost all of them either saying "Esther is gentle" or "Esther is kind."

We thank You for the depth of the relationship she enjoyed with You. As she wrote those screeds to You, it must have thrilled Your heart to hear Your child finish her prayers at night with "Love You lots and lots" as she gave herself to sleep.

The Road Not Chosen

We thank You for her quirky sense of humour that emerged best when she felt safe. Her gentle wit and razor sharp insight into people around her simply delighted us so often.

We thank You for the caring side of her nature which caused her to go out in love and concern for the disadvantaged, for people in her world who were just a little unusual, and for the elderly. She made these people feel that they mattered.

We thank You for her courage and spirit of adventure. You gave us a daughter who, like Abraham, was never afraid to take bold initiatives, even if they meant leaving the familiarity of home and friendships. Despite her shyness she bravely embarked on adventures which deepened her character and tested her walk with You. We want to emulate her initiative.

We thank You for her determination to improve herself in those life areas that are most significant – in spirituality, in academic study, in music and in fitness. We feel privileged to have been trusted with a daughter who had the courage to face deeply personal challenges, like her anxiety about speaking, and not shy away from facing these hurdles. By drawing on Your power, she overcame some of her greatest obstacles. Her conscientiousness and hard work were an example to us.

We thank You for the faithfulness and loyalty she displayed in her friendships.

We thank You for the way she sought to live a highly principled life, even to her own disadvantage. Her wrestling with the place of Law and Grace deepened her enormously and must have brought joy to Your heart.

We thank You that she embraced the musical gift You invested in her from her earliest days. Although she was so rarely heard in public, we believe You were thrilled with the intensity of her praise and the clarity of her voice as she worshipped You at the altar of her own heart and in the privacy of her own room.

Heaven Day

We thank You for the joy she gave to us over each of the twenty-two years she was part of our family. We felt loved by her even though she often found it tough to express her affection in words.

We thank You for her respect for Christopher. In their growing closeness over the last few years, You gave her a much deeper confidence as a sister and enjoyment in their relationship together. Despite her shyness, we were so pleased to see the enjoyment and natural pride which filled her as a bridesmaid at his wedding.

Thank You for the love which You gave us for her as her parents. We feel as if that specific love can never be diverted elsewhere, and her loss leaves us with a soul-emptiness which we only slowly come to terms with. We need to experience Your healing and receive Your resilience as we continue through life without our daughter.

We confess that You have surprised us by the brevity of her life but we thank You that the longings we brought to You at her dedication have all been fulfilled in her short life. We want to tell You that we are grateful she is now in Your presence enjoying joy and freedom, and the struggles which plagued her on earth are finally a thing of the past. The race she ran with such perseverance is now over.

We trust You Lord that in Your goodness You know the glory she's been saved into, and in Your mercy the trials she's been saved from.

We recognise that the past few years have been a consistent struggle for her but You never left her side, You never let her down, and You were present even when she was slipping into unconsciousness.

And so we want to commit ourselves wholeheartedly to You for the rest of our own earthly race, however long it may be.

The Road Not Chosen

We want to tell You that we love You and desire to receive the legacy of persevering love for God that Esther has bequeathed to us.

We want to make our relationship with You the primary focus of our lives. So lead us only into those activities and relationships that are ordained by You and will be anointed by You.

Work through us to bring many other people to know You. When we meet challenges, small or large, help us to tackle them as our daughter did, with wisdom and grace. Deepen our love for You and our Christian character during these difficult times.

So we rejoice that for our daughter Esther every day is now a Heaven Day.

Amen.

Bible verses for you to think about

In cards, e-mails, texts and Facebook posts, our friends shared numerous passages from the Bible they thought would help us in our tragedy. We have collected most of them here because they became a source of great comfort and strength at moments when our sense of loss was at its most intense. Every verse or passage is a gift from someone, which they have thought carefully about giving us; and that makes them a unique collection of Bible verses. We have returned to them many times since, when we have needed to realign our minds to God's purpose and draw His comfort from them. They became a source of great personal strength to us in our journey of grieving.

We have left them in biblical order because any other sequence seemed forced. Each one applies in a different way; some encourage us to be strong and brave while others urge us to let it all out to the Lord. Some speak to our situation while others refer to Esther herself. But we realised that we had here a collection of concentrated biblical source material that was laced with tenderness and oozed strength.

We hope you will find them to be the same if you are facing a loss of your own:

> Numbers 6:26: The Lord turn his face towards you and give you peace.

> Deuteronomy 32:3-4: I will proclaim the name of the Lord. Oh, praise the greatness of our God! He is the Rock, his works are perfect, and all his ways are just. A faithful God who does no wrong, upright and just is he.

Deuteronomy 33:12: Let the beloved of the Lord rest secure in him, for he shields him all day long, and the one the Lord loves rests between his shoulders.

Deuteronomy 33:27: The eternal God is your refuge, and underneath are the everlasting arms.

Joshua 1:5: No-one will be able to stand up against you all the days of your life. As I was with Moses, so I will be with you; I will never leave you nor forsake you.

2 Samuel 22:2-3: [King David] said, "The Lord is my rock, my fortress and my deliverer; my God is my rock, in whom I take refuge, my shield and the horn of my salvation. He is my stronghold, my refuge and my saviour – from violent men you save me."

2 Samuel 22:31-33: As for God, his way is perfect; the word of the Lord is flawless. He is a shield for all who take refuge in him. For who is God besides the Lord? And who is the Rock except our God? It is God who arms me with strength and makes my way perfect.

Nehemiah 8:10: Nehemiah said, "Go and enjoy choice food and sweet drinks, and send some to those who have nothing prepared. This day is sacred to our Lord. Do not grieve, for the joy of the Lord is your strength."

Job 5:8-11: But if it were I, I would appeal to God; I would lay my cause before him. He performs wonders that cannot be fathomed, miracles that cannot be counted. He bestows rain on the earth; he sends water upon the countryside. The lowly he sets on high, and those who mourn are lifted to safety.

Psalm 23:1-6: The Lord is my shepherd, I shall not be in want. He makes me lie down in green pastures, he leads me beside quiet waters, he restores my soul. He guides me in paths of righteousness for his name's sake. Even though I walk through the valley of the shadow of death, I will fear no evil, for you are with me; your rod and your staff, they comfort me. You prepare a table before me in the presence of my enemies. You anoint my head with oil; my cup overflows. Surely goodness and love will follow me all the days of my life, and I will dwell in the house of the Lord for ever.

Psalm 27:14: Wait for the Lord; be strong and take heart and wait for the Lord.

Psalm 29:11: The Lord gives strength to his people; the Lord blesses his people with peace.

Psalm 31:1: In you, O Lord, I have taken refuge; let me never be put to shame; deliver me in your righteousness.

Psalm 34:18: The Lord is close to the broken-hearted and saves those who are crushed in spirit.

Psalm 37:4-5: Delight yourself in the Lord and he will give you the desires of your heart. Commit your way to the Lord; trust in him and he will do this.

Psalm 46:1-3, 46:10-11: God is our refuge and strength, an ever-present help in trouble. Therefore we will not fear, though the earth give way and the mountains fall into the heart of the sea, though its waters roar and foam and the mountains quake with their surging. ... Be still, and know that I am God; I will be exalted among the nations, I will be exalted in the earth. The Lord Almighty is with us; the God of Jacob is our fortress.

The Road Not Chosen

Psalm 55:22: Cast your cares on the Lord and he will sustain you; he will never let the righteous fall.

Psalm 57:2-3: I cry out to God Most High, to God, who fulfils [his purpose] for me. He sends from heaven and saves me, rebuking those who hotly pursue me; God sends his love and his faithfulness.

Psalm 61:4: I long to dwell in your tent for ever and take refuge in the shelter of your wings.

Psalm 62:1-2: My soul finds rest in God alone; my salvation comes from him. He alone is my rock and my salvation; he is my fortress, I shall never be shaken.

Psalm 68:19: Praise be to the Lord, to God our Saviour, who daily bears our burdens.

Psalm 71:1-3: In you, O Lord, I have taken refuge; let me never be put to shame. Rescue me and deliver me in your righteousness; turn your ear to me and save me. Be my rock of refuge, to which I can always go; give the command to save me, for you are my rock and my fortress.

Psalm 91:4: He will cover you with his feathers, and under his wings you will find refuge; his faithfulness will be your shield and rampart.

Psalm 94:19: When anxiety was great within me, your consolation brought joy to my soul.

Psalm 116:5: The Lord is gracious and righteous; our God is full of compassion.

Psalm 116:15: Precious in the sight of the Lord is the death of his saints.

Bible verses for you to think about

Psalm 119:76: May your unfailing love be my comfort, according to your promise to your servant.

Psalm 121:2: My help comes from the Lord, the Maker of heaven and earth.

Psalm 125:2: As the mountains surround Jerusalem, so the Lord surrounds his people both now and for evermore.

Psalm 139:16-18: Your eyes saw my unformed body. All the days ordained for me were written in your book before one of them came to be. How precious to me are your thoughts, O God! How vast is the sum of them! Were I to count them, they would outnumber the grains of sand. When I awake, I am still with you.

Psalm 145:18: The Lord is near to all who call on him, to all who call on him in truth.

Psalm 147:5: Great is our Lord and mighty in power; his understanding has no limit.

Proverbs 3:5: Trust in the Lord with all your heart and lean not on your own understanding.

Proverbs 4:18: The path of the righteous is like the first gleam of dawn, shining ever brighter till the full light of day.

Isaiah 40:31: Those who hope in the Lord will renew their strength. They will soar on wings like eagles; they will run and not grow weary, they will walk and not be faint.

Isaiah 41:10: So do not fear, for I am with you; do not be dismayed, for I am your God. I will strengthen you and help you; I will uphold you with my righteous right hand.

The Road Not Chosen

Isaiah 41:13: For I am the Lord, your God, who takes hold of your right hand and says to you, "Do not fear; I will help you."

Isaiah 55:8-9: "For my thoughts are not your thoughts, neither are your ways my ways," declares the Lord. "As the heavens are higher than the earth, so are my ways higher than your ways and my thoughts than your thoughts."

Isaiah 58:11: The Lord will guide you always; he will satisfy your needs in a sun-scorched land and will strengthen your frame. You will be like a well-watered garden, like a spring whose waters never fail.

Isaiah 63:9: In all their distress he too was distressed, and the angel of his presence saved them. In his love and mercy he redeemed them; he lifted them up and carried them all the days of old.

Jeremiah 29:11: "I know the plans I have for you," declares the Lord, "plans to prosper you and not to harm you, plans to give you hope and a future."

Lamentations 3:22-23: It is because of the Lord's great love we are not consumed, for his compassions never fail. They are new every morning; great is your faithfulness.

Matthew 5:4: [Jesus said] "Blessed are those who mourn, for they will be comforted."

Matthew 11:28: [Jesus said] "Come to me, all you who are weary and burdened, and I will give you rest."

John 10:27-28: [Jesus said] "My sheep listen to my voice; I know them, and they follow me. I give them eternal life, and they shall never perish; no-one can snatch them out of my hand."

Bible verses for you to think about

John 11:17-44: "Where have you laid Lazarus?" Jesus asked. "Come and see, Lord," they replied. At that moment Jesus wept. Then the Jews said, "See how he loved him!"

John 14:27: [Jesus said] "Peace I leave with you; my peace I give you. I do not give to you as the world gives. Do not let your hearts be troubled and do not be afraid."

John 16:33: [Jesus said] "I have told you these things, so that in me you may have peace. In this world you will have trouble. But take heart! I have overcome the world."

Romans 8:37-39: In all these things we are more than conquerors through him who loved us. For I am convinced that neither death nor life, neither angels nor demons, neither the present nor the future, nor any powers, neither height nor depth, nor anything else in all creation, will be able to separate us from the love of God that is in Christ Jesus our Lord.

1 Corinthians 2:9: It is written: "No eye has seen, no ear has heard, no mind has conceived what God has prepared for those who love him."

1 Corinthians 13:8: Love never fails. But where there are prophecies, they will cease; where there are tongues, they will be stilled; where there is knowledge, it will pass away.

2 Corinthians 1:3-5: Praise be to the God and Father of our Lord Jesus Christ, the Father of compassion and the God of all comfort, who comforts us in all our troubles, so that we can comfort those in any trouble with the comfort we ourselves have received from God. For just as the sufferings of Christ flow over into

our lives, so also through Christ our comfort overflows.

2 Corinthians 12:9: [God] said to me, "My grace is sufficient for you, for my power is made perfect in weakness." Therefore I will boast all the more gladly about my weaknesses, so that Christ's power may rest on me.

Philippians 4:7: And the peace of God, which transcends all understanding, will guard your hearts and your minds in Christ Jesus.

Colossians 1:3: We always thank God, the Father of our Lord Jesus Christ, when we pray for you.

2 Thessalonians 2:16-17: May our Lord Jesus Christ himself and God our Father, who loved us and by his grace gave us eternal encouragement and good hope, encourage your hearts and strengthen you in every good deed and word.

Hebrews 6:18-20: God did this so that, by two unchangeable things in which it is impossible for God to lie, we who have fled to take hold of the hope offered to us may be greatly encouraged. We have this hope as an anchor for the soul, firm and secure. It enters the inner sanctuary behind the curtain, where Jesus, who went before us, has entered on our behalf. He has become a high priest for ever, in the order of Melchizedek.

Revelation 7:17: For the Lamb at the centre of the throne will be their shepherd; he will lead them to springs of living water. And God will wipe away every tear from their eyes.

Bible verses for you to think about

Revelation 21:4: He will wipe every tear from their eyes. There will be no more death or mourning or crying or pain, for the old order of things has passed away.

Additional Resources

Care for the Family

Care for the Family run the Bereaved Parents' Network to help those who are living with loss to discover hope for the future, and the strength to rebuild their lives and the lives of their families. They also provide a variety of articles and resources about grieving.

http://www.careforthefamily.org.uk/family-life/bereavement-support

Alpha Publications

While best known for the Christian basics course Alpha, this organisation has other resources including *The Bereavement Journey*, a six-week course, providing community and support for people who have experienced a loss. The filmed sessions are accompanied by guest notes, which provide a summary of themes as well as discussion prompts. All the resources can be accessed directly from the website:

http://shop.alpha.org/product/364/bereavement-journey

National Health Service

The NHS can offer bereavement support and counselling. Referral to NHS services is normally done through your local GP who will be involved if you need to take time off work. The introductory information is here:

http://www.nhs.uk/Livewell/bereavement/Pages/bereaveme nt.aspx

Winston's Wish

Winston's Wish is the leading childhood bereavement charity in the UK. They offer practical support and guidance to bereaved children, their families and professionals.

http://www.winstonswish.org.uk/

Cruse

Cruse Bereavement Care's vision is that all bereaved people have somewhere to turn to when someone dies. Their mission is to offer support, advice and information to children, young people and adults following a bereavement.

Cruse provides training for external organisations and for those who may encounter bereaved people in the course of their work.

http://www.cruse.org.uk/

Books for bereaved parents

Gloria Hunniford, *Always With You* (Hodder and Stoughton: London, 2008)

Harriet Sarnoff Schiff, *The Bereaved Parent* (Penguin Books: New York, 1978)

Sarah Williams, *The Shaming of the Strong* (Kingsway Publications: Eastbourne, 2006)*

Nicholas Wolterstorff, *Lament for a Son* (Eerdmans: Grand Rapids, 1987)

General bereavement books

Sandra Aldrich, *Living through the loss of someone you love* (Regal Books: Ventura, 1995)*

Carol W Cornish, *The Undistracted Widow* (Crossway: Wheaton, 2010)*

John W James and Russell Friedman, *The Grief Recovery Handbook* (Harper Collins: New York, 2009)

C S Lewis, *A Grief Observed* (Faber & Faber: London, 2013)*

Pablo Martinez and Ali Hull, *Tracing the Rainbow* (Spring Harvest Publishing/Authentic Media: Milton Keynes, 2004)*

Jerry Sittser, *A Grace Disguised* (Zondervan: Grand Rapids, 2004)*

The Road Not Chosen

Alison Wertheimer, *A Special Scar* (Routledge: Hove, 2001)

Books marked with an asterisk (*) are written from a Christian perspective.